THE
ASIAN
PANTRY

To my mum for buying me my first bottle of sweet chilli and for keeping my Asian pantry well stocked ever since.

The Asian Pantry

Quick & easy everyday dishes using big Asian flavours

Dominique Woolf

Photography by Uyen Luu
Illustrations by Sandra Isaksson

MICHAEL JOSEPH

contents

intro.

The pantry, storecupboard, larder. Call it what you want, this is where it all begins.

My pantry is part of me. If I could take it away with me when I go on holiday, I would (just ask my husband and he would agree!). Bottles, jars, condiments, pastes, oils, spices. You name it, I probably have it. But your pantry doesn't have to be heaving to be effective and, in this book, I've chosen just 21 key Asian ingredients that are all you need in order to whip up a gorgeous meal any day of the week. It might sound like a lot, but the chances are you have many of them already.

If you have a copy of my first book, *Dominique's Kitchen*, you'll know that my recipes always have big flavour at the heart of them, but I also always strive to make them reliable and easy to make. So many of you wrote to me saying you had never cooked so much from one book because of just that.

In *The Asian Pantry*, I wanted to keep the same promise and take it a step further, make things even simpler. Stunning food cooked with minimal fuss. Big, vibrant, feisty flavours that transport you across the globe (or at least to a buzzy restaurant!) and that anyone can recreate.

That's where the pantry comes in. With these key ingredients to hand, you'll be able to throw together a mouth-watering meal in less time than it takes to scroll through a takeaway menu – whether it's Monday night and the last thing you want to do is cook, or it's Friday and you fancy something a bit more special but don't want to spend all evening in the kitchen.

By focusing on the ingredients list this book also helps the storecupboard work for you. If you buy an ingredient such as a Thai red curry paste, for example, you'll be able to find several recipes to help use it up, meaning less waste and more deliciousness!

Being half-Thai, Asian food is my lifeblood, but it's not just the traditional cuisine I love. For me, it's about those incredible flavours – spicy, salty, sour, sweet and umami – that add so much to a dish. Yes, you'll find recipes in this book that are based on more 'traditional' dishes – always with my spin put on, of course. But you'll also find many recipes which use the ingredients in exciting and unexpected ways to create something quite unique – all the while being truly achievable.

The Asian Pantry is a collection of recipes that I hope will transform your midweek meals and inject a little magic into your everyday. Come with me on a journey through flavour while never leaving your kitchen!

Dominique

My Top Tips for Recipe Success

Before you get cooking, have a read through my top tips for recipe success. A little bit of advance prep will get you a LONG way and will ensure that every meal that you cook is as stress-free to make as it is delicious!

Read the recipe *before* starting

Hands up who's been caught out by not doing this? I certainly have! Read the whole recipe from start to finish before you start cooking to ensure the best possible recipe success.

Prep your ingredients

Just a note that the prep is listed in the ingredients section so read through the recipe (see point above!) and get everything out and ready to go. This will make the cooking process a lot easier and less frantic!

Taste test

So important when cooking anything, especially Asian cuisine. You know what you like, so taste and adjust as you go (starting with small amounts).

Use up your fridge

I'm a big fan of using up your fridge. Most of the recipes are flexible, so use whatever veg or protein component you happen to have on hand. Just try to use approximately the same amount and adjust cooking times where necessary.

Kitchen Essentials

I'm not a great believer in filling your kitchen drawers or cupboards with hundreds of expensive gadgets that you won't use. These are my essentials.

Knife

A large chef's knife is a must for me. I use mine for pretty much everything, whether fruit, veg, meat, fish, herbs – you name it. It doesn't have to be expensive but will make the prep much easier. It does need to be kept sharp, so think about investing in a sharpening steel or knife sharpener.

Non-stick pan

A large non-stick frying pan or wok is essential if you want an easy life!

Measuring spoons

No more guesstimating quantities with dubiously heaped spoonfuls!

Fine grater

E.g. Microplane. Essential for ginger. I find this much more effective than using a normal grater.

Mini whisk

I use this for making dressings and sauces, especially useful with thicker ingredients like miso paste or peanut butter.

Julienne peeler

Perfect for cutting carrots into thin strips.

My Asian Pantry

Listed below are the 21 essential Asian pantry ingredients that the recipes in this book are built around. Most are readily available in a large supermarket with a well-stocked international food aisle, but I've also suggested some simple substitutes where possible. Rather than go out and buy all 21, why not have a look through the book and plan which meals you want to cook – the chances are that you'll find that a lot of them share ingredients. All of these should keep happily in your storecupboard or fridge for several months, but always check the individual packaging for storage instructions.

Chilli bean paste/sauce

This is sold under various names including doubanjiang, toban djan, Sichuan chilli bean sauce, toban chilli bean sauce and Sichuan broad bean paste. A salty, spicy, garlicky cooking ingredient made from fermented soybeans, broad beans, garlic and chillies, it gives a savoury, umami-filled depth to dishes. I use Lee Kum Kee chilli bean sauce, which is less salty than some others – if using another brand then start off with less. Available online or in Asian supermarkets.

> **SWITCH**
>
> *If you can't get hold of chilli bean paste, then substitute equal parts sriracha and white miso paste. It won't be exactly the same but will give you garlic heat, salt and umaminess.*

Chilli flakes

Dried red chilli flakes add a roasted flavour to dishes. They can be used in place of fresh chillies if you don't have any to hand. Start with ¼ tsp for each chilli and add from there. Unlike chilli powder, these flakes are not mixed with other ingredients.

Chinese 5-spice

A traditional blend of five aromatic spices commonly used in Chinese cuisine, typically including star anise, cinnamon, fennel seeds, black pepper and cloves. It adds depth and complexity to dishes as well as a distinctive aromatic layer of flavour. Also available as a 'seasoning' mix with added ingredients such as salt, onion and garlic powder – this is fine for savoury dishes but to be avoided when using in desserts.

Coconut milk

Most brands tend to be a bit gloopy due to the use of stabilizers combined with a low percentage of coconut milk/extract. They're fine to use, but if you are able to get hold of one with at least

60 per cent coconut extract, or one which has no extra additives, such as Biona, then all the better. I always use full-fat coconut milk as I far prefer the taste and texture compared to the light version. Bear in mind that in colder months, coconut milk tends to set solid. If this is the case, place the open can in hot water for 5–10 minutes, stirring occasionally, until loosened. Leftover coconut milk can be frozen.

Crispy chilli oil with bits

My favourite condiment and a brilliant ingredient too. We're after flavour and texture, not just oil – so get one with lots of bits! I always use my own award-winning version called Chilli Crunch, available from The Woolf's Kitchen.

 SWITCH If you can't get hold of any, then try my recipe for Easy Chilli Oil with Bits on page 194.

Curry powder

I tend to use a basic, medium-heat curry powder, but feel free to use whichever heat you prefer.

Desiccated coconut

The grated and dried flesh of the coconut. Great for adding a subtle coconut flavour to both sweet and savoury dishes. For the recipes in this book, if possible, opt for the unsweetened variety and avoid desiccated coconut labelled as 'fine', as it won't provide the right texture.

Fish sauce

An essential ingredient and condiment in Southeast Asian cuisine. Made from fermented fish and salt, it has a pungent smell and a salty, umami-rich flavour.

 SWITCH For a veggie or vegan alternative, in most cases you can simply swap the fish sauce for light soy. For salad dressings, I would recommend using an equal mix of light soy and rice vinegar instead. You can also buy vegetarian fish sauce.

Gochujang

A traditional Korean chilli paste made from red chillies, fermented soybeans and glutinous rice, amongst other things. This deep red paste adds a unique and complex spicy, sweet-savoury flavour to dishes. Available in some major supermarkets, as well as Asian shops and online.

 SWITCH If you can't get hold of it, then substitute sriracha instead. The flavour profile is different but will add similar heat and umaminess.

Hoisin sauce

A thick, dark, sweet and savoury sauce made from soybeans, garlic, chilli, vinegar and spices. Popular in both Chinese and Vietnamese cuisine, not only as a condiment (crispy duck pancakes and summer rolls here we come!), but also as a versatile cooking ingredient used in stir-fries, sauces and marinades.

Noodles

Having a large stash of noodles in the cupboard means a meal is never far away. I tend to use a mixture of dried and ready-to-wok. Dried includes rice noodles (both flat and vermicelli) as well as noodles of the egg, wheat, and ramen variety. Ready-to-wok includes udon and wheat noodles (both thin and medium). Most recipes will work with any type if you don't have the stated one to hand – just check the packet instructions for timings.

Oyster sauce

Made from oyster extracts, soy sauce, sugar and seasonings, this is a core ingredient in Thai and Chinese cuisine. Savoury and umami-rich, it adds a rounded saltiness and depth to dishes.

 For a veggie/vegan alternative try using a vegetarian stir-fry sauce – both Lee Kum Kee and Amoy make one.

Rice

The core staple at the heart of Asian cuisine. Jasmine, used in Thailand, is my favourite variety because of the stickier texture. However, basmati works just as well for most recipes.

Rice vinegar

Made from fermented rice, this vinegar is milder and more delicate than other varieties, with a subtle acidity and sweetness.

 Although my preference in this book, in most recipes you can substitute it for white wine vinegar, apple cider vinegar or red wine vinegar.

Soy sauce

I use light soy sauce, which is thinner and less heavy than the dark variety, but full of flavour.

 For a gluten-free version use tamari instead. You can also buy lower-salt varieties if you're trying to cut down on sodium in your diet.

Sriracha

The beloved Thai hot chilli sauce made from fermented chillies, vinegar, garlic, sugar and salt. Adds a fiery garlicky kick, along with tanginess and a slight sweetness. Used the world over for dipping, drizzling and as a cooking ingredient.

If you can't get hold of any, then try using another hot sauce (ideally one with garlic in it) or gochujang (see page 16), depending on the dish.

Tahini

A paste made from ground sesame seeds, boasting a nutty flavour and creamy texture.

Tamarind paste

Derived from the flesh of the tamarind fruit, this paste lends a tangy, slightly sweet flavour to dishes. Available in both tubs and jars, there are two distinct varieties – a more watery brown variety (which is the one I use), and a tar-like inky black version, which is far more concentrated. Both can be labelled as either tamarind paste or tamarind concentrate, making it hard to decipher which one to buy, so please assess based on colour and texture. If you can only get hold of the more concentrated version, simply use ⅓ of the amount called for, and make up the rest of the amount with water, i.e. 1 tbsp of tamarind paste = 1 tsp tamarind concentrate + 2 tsp water.

Thai curry paste – green and red

I would highly recommend buying a good-quality Thai brand paste such as Mae Ploy, available from some major supermarkets, all Asian shops

and online. The flavour is far superior. If you're unable to get hold of one, then be sure to taste the dish as you go – you may need to add more paste and/or seasoning and chilli to compensate. For a vegan version, try Thai Taste.

White miso paste

A traditional Japanese seasoning made from fermented soybeans, rice or barley, and salt. It lends umami depth and complexity to dishes, both savoury and sweet. There are several different types available but for the purpose of these recipes I have used 'white miso'. You can also use products labelled just 'miso' (light brown in colour and comparable in strength to white miso).

A Note on Fresh Ingredients

As well as my pantry ingredients, there is a handful of fresh ingredients that I always make sure I have a healthy supply of. These all add an immediate punch of vibrant flavour to any dish and can be stored in the freezer, meaning that you never have to worry about them going bad at the bottom of the fridge.

Chillies

Red chillies – when listed in a recipe, these refer to the standard mild red chillies you buy in the supermarket or greengrocer's. The heat level is mild to medium. Deseed if you prefer it milder.

Bird's-eye chilli – a small red chilli used in Thai cuisine. Much hotter than the standard red chilli. Feel free to swap to the standard red if you prefer less heat.

All fresh chillies can be frozen and used straight from the freezer.

Garlic

An essential ingredient in many of the dishes in this book.

I go through a huge amount and tend to keep it in the fridge to maintain freshness, but it can be frozen as whole bulbs (if in good condition) or as peeled cloves. Can be used from frozen.

Ginger

If the skin is in good condition, I don't tend to peel it. A fine grater such as a Microplane makes grating much easier. Fresh ginger can be frozen either with the skin on, or peeled and trimmed if necessary, and then grated from frozen.

Lemongrass

Fresh lemongrass stalks can be frozen. If using whole, allow to defrost and soften a little before bashing. If slicing, they can be sliced from frozen.

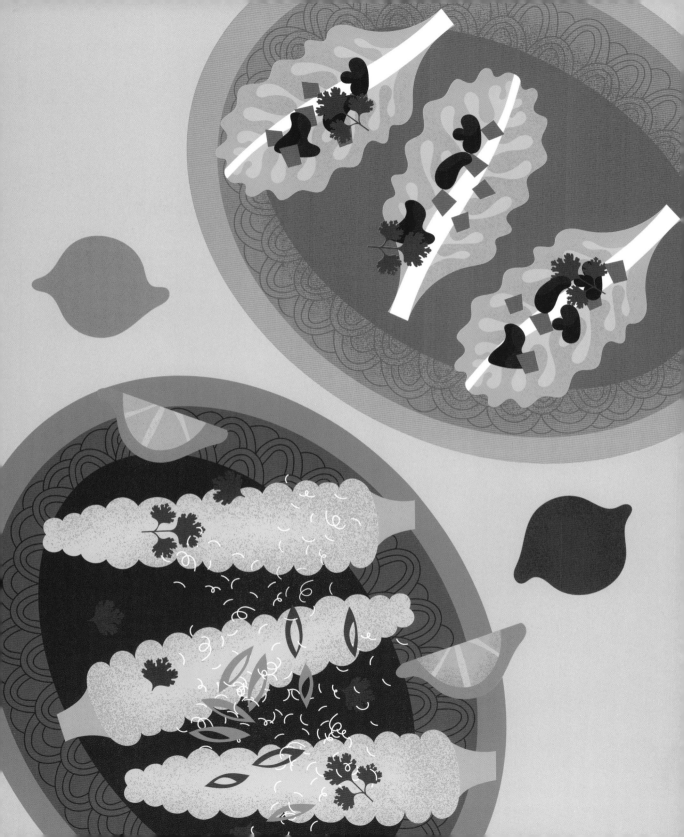

small plates

Crispy Pork Belly Wraps with Watermelon Salad

Serves:
4

Prep:
15 mins

Cook:
20 mins

500g rindless pork belly slices, cut into 1cm pieces
neutral oil, to fry

For the sauce
3 tbsp gochujang
3 tbsp hoisin sauce
3 tbsp ketchup
1 tbsp rice vinegar

For the salad
450g watermelon (unpeeled weight, or 275g peeled weight), cut into 2cm cubes
1 tbsp rice vinegar
½ tsp sugar
½ tsp fish sauce
a handful of fresh coriander leaves
a handful of fresh mint leaves, shredded
sea salt flakes

To serve
2 heads of little gem lettuce, leaves separated

If I saw this dish on a menu, I'd order it in a flash. Crispy bites of pork belly, slathered in a spicy, sticky hoisin and gochujang sauce, served in crisp lettuce leaves, and all topped off with a herby watermelon salad. Hello!

Boiling the pork before frying renders away some of the fat, giving all the golden crunchiness without hours of cooking. The sublime Korean-style sauce is a match made in foodie heaven, while the watermelon salad adds a refreshing contrast.

Bring a large pan of water to the boil over a high heat, then add the pork belly and reduce the heat to medium. Simmer gently for 10 minutes.

Meanwhile make the sauce by combining all the ingredients in a small bowl.

Once the pork is cooked, drain and air-dry in the sieve or colander over the pan, then dry thoroughly with kitchen paper. You want it to be as dry as possible. If you are doing this in advance you can also refrigerate it to help dry it out.

Once dry, heat a large frying pan or wok over a high heat and add a drizzle of oil. Carefully tip in the pork belly and reduce the heat to medium. Stir-fry for around 5 minutes, or until the pork is crispy and golden all over. Remove the excess fat from the pan, then pour in half the sauce. Stir to coat and turn the heat off.

Just before serving, make the watermelon salad. Put the watermelon into a bowl and add the vinegar, sugar, fish sauce, coriander and mint, along with a pinch of salt. Mix to combine.

Place the lettuce leaves on a platter and spoon in the pork, with a drizzle more sauce if desired. Top with a little of the watermelon salad and serve.

Spicy Tuna Crispy Rice

Serves:
4

Prep:
5 mins

Cook:
25 mins

Makes:
16 squares

Chilling:
+ 30 mins
chilling

For the rice

150g jasmine rice, unrinsed

½ tsp salt

1 tbsp rice vinegar

neutral oil, to fry

For the tuna

1 x 145g tin of tuna, drained

3 tbsp mayo

1 tbsp sriracha, plus extra
to drizzle

30g cornichons, sliced,
plus 1 tbsp of their
pickling liquor

¼ of a cucumber, sliced

Crispy, crunchy, chewy rice topped with spicy, creamy tuna. This is my twist on the Nobu-famous dish, using tinned tuna in place of sushi-grade tuna. Sriracha, mayo and sweet pickled cornichons elevate the humble storecupboard hero to new heights, making a simple but highly effective topping for the moreish fried rice. Usually made with Japanese sushi rice – a short-grain, very sticky rice – this version uses the more widely available jasmine variety. It does need to be chilled before frying, but otherwise it is easy to prepare. An enticing mouthful that always gets a 'wow' from guests!

Place the rice in a small pan with 275ml of water and the salt. Stir to combine. Bring to a boil, uncovered over a high heat, then place the lid on and reduce the heat to low. Cook for 12 minutes, until the rice is cooked. Take off the heat and leave to steam with the lid on for 5 minutes.

Meanwhile, line a baking tin (approx. 20 x 20cm) with baking paper or clingfilm.

Once the rice is cooked, drizzle over the rice vinegar and combine. Spoon into the baking tin using the back of a spatula or wooden spoon. You may need to wet the spatula or spoon in between spoonfuls. Press firmly – you want it tightly packed, with a depth of around 1½cm. Once cool, cover with a sheet of baking paper or clingfilm and place in the freezer for 30–60 minutes to firm up (or in the fridge for 2 hours or overnight), then slice into 16 squares.

While the rice is chilling, combine the tuna, mayo, sriracha, cornichons and the cornichon liquor in a bowl and set aside.

Heat a large non-stick frying pan over a medium-high heat. Add 2 tablespoons of oil and when hot, add half of the rice squares to the pan. Make sure they don't touch. Cook for 3–4 minutes on each side, until golden, being careful not to break the pieces when you turn them over. You may need to add a little more oil. Place on kitchen paper to drain. Repeat with the remaining rice.

To assemble, simply place a slice of cucumber on each piece of
rice, followed by a spoonful of the tuna mix and a drizzle of sriracha.
Serve immediately.

Zingy Garlic & Ginger Chickpea Tacos

Serves:	Prep:	Cook:
4	15 mins	15 mins

For the chickpeas
neutral oil, to fry

6cm piece of fresh ginger, peeled and cut into very fine matchsticks

2 large cloves of garlic, roughly chopped

1 x 400g tin of chickpeas, drained, and dried well

sea salt flakes

1 tsp curry powder (whichever heat preferred)

½ a red onion, finely chopped

2 tbsp shop-bought crispy onions

2–3 tbsp salted peanuts, chopped

a handful of fresh coriander leaves, roughly chopped

a handful of fresh mint leaves, shredded

For the cabbage
200g white cabbage, finely shredded

4 tbsp mayo

2 tsp lime juice (approx. ½ a lime)

1 tsp sriracha

For the dressing
4 tbsp fresh lime juice (approx. 2½–3 limes)

1½ tbsp light soy sauce

1½ tbsp soft brown sugar

1 bird's-eye or mild red chilli, finely chopped (deseed for a milder heat)

To serve
8 small tortillas

These are chickpeas, but not as you know them! Pan-fried with spices until gorgeously crispy, then dressed with a zappy lime, chilli and soy dressing, their earthy notes work perfectly with all that zing. Delicious on their own as a salad, they're even better piled into tacos with a creamy slaw.

Heat 2 tablespoons of oil in a large frying pan over a medium-high heat. When hot, fry the ginger for 1–2 minutes, until crispy, then remove with a slotted spoon on to kitchen paper. Add the garlic and a bit more oil if needed, and fry for another 1–2 minutes, until just golden, stirring often. Take the pan off the heat and remove the garlic with a slotted spoon, leaving the oil. Ensure no bits are left to prevent burning. Place on kitchen paper.

Add another 1–2 tablespoons of oil to the pan and when hot add the chickpeas with a pinch of salt. Fry for 8–10 minutes, tossing occasionally.

While the chickpeas are cooking, combine the ingredients for the cabbage in a bowl and set aside.

Combine the ingredients for the dressing in a small bowl.

Once the chickpeas are golden and crispy, sprinkle over the curry powder and combine well. Cook for another 30–60 seconds, then remove from the heat and tip into a large mixing bowl.

Just before serving, add the chopped red onion, crispy fried onions, salted peanuts and reserved garlic and ginger to the chickpeas. Mix in the coriander and mint, followed by most of the dressing.

To serve, warm the tortillas and top each one with a little of the cabbage and spoonfuls of the chickpeas, and serve with the remaining dressing on the side. Eat immediately.

The dressing will soften the crispy chickpeas, so don't add it all at once, and be sure to dress at the last minute, just before serving.

TIP

Citrussy Smoked Salmon 'Tartare'

Serves:	Prep:	Cook:
4	10 mins	0 mins

4 tbsp lime juice (approx. 2–3 limes)

zest of 2 limes

2 tbsp orange juice

2 tsp rice vinegar

½ tsp light soy sauce

¼ of a red onion, finely chopped

½–1 red chilli, finely chopped (deseed for a milder heat)

200g smoked salmon, chopped into roughly 2cm pieces

1 ripe avocado, cut into small cubes

a handful of fresh coriander, roughly chopped

To serve

prawn crackers

Alive with the bright, citrussy zing of both lime and orange juice, a spicy kick from chilli, creamy avocado and fragrant coriander, this no-cook starter is an explosion of flavour.

Ready in just a few minutes, it's a perfect dish for fuss-free entertaining (or simply a delicious starter for yourself!).

In a mixing bowl, combine the lime juice and zest, orange juice, vinegar, soy, onion and chilli. Add the smoked salmon and avocado and gently combine.

Mix in the coriander and place on a serving dish. Serve immediately, with prawn crackers on the side.

Fried Courgettes with Fish Sauce Caramel

Serves:
4 as a sharing plate

Prep:
5 mins

Cook:
15 mins

4 tbsp cornflour
¼ tsp fine salt
2 large courgettes,
   (approx. 250g each)
   cut into batons
neutral oil, to fry

For the fish sauce caramel
4 tbsp soft brown sugar
2 tbsp water
2 tsp fish sauce

To serve
sea salt flakes

Fish sauce caramel?! I hear you say! If you like your sweet-savoury combinations then you have to try this. The salty, umami notes of the fish sauce work so well with the caramel, elevating the humble courgette to a whole new level of deliciousness. If you're anything like us, you'll be fighting to scrape the plate clean! Although I would highly recommend trying it with fish sauce, it also works well with soy.

The cheat's caramel is as easy as it gets. Simply simmer the ingredients in a pan until the sugar dissolves and the sauce thickens.

Place the cornflour and salt in a shallow dish and combine. Add the courgettes and coat well.

Heat 2 tablespoons of oil in a large non-stick frying pan over a medium-high heat. When very hot, add the courgettes, leaving behind any excess cornflour. You will need to do this in batches. Leave for a couple of minutes or so before turning, to make sure a golden crust forms. Cook until golden all over, then remove and place on kitchen paper to drain. Repeat with all the courgettes.

While the courgettes are cooking, make the fish sauce caramel. Place the ingredients in a small saucepan over a medium heat. Stir to dissolve the sugar, then bubble gently until it becomes syrupy.

Put the courgettes on a serving dish and sprinkle with sea salt flakes, then drizzle over the fish sauce caramel. Serve immediately.

Udon Gyoza with Citrus Chilli Oil

Serves:
3–4
Makes:
8–10
gyoza

Prep:
10 mins

Cook:
10 mins

These Japanese pan-fried dumplings are a kind of cheat's version of a gyoza, using ready-cooked udon noodles, along with minced meat, garlic, ginger and spring onions. The udon noodles are the star, creating a wonderful texture that manages to be chewy yet golden and crispy at the same time. The citrus chilli oil is entirely optional but really takes the dish to the next level.

Combine the ingredients for the citrus chilli oil in a small bowl and set aside.

Chop the udon noodles into roughly 2cm pieces. Place them in a mixing bowl with the rest of the gyoza ingredients and combine well.

Heat a large non-stick frying pan over a medium heat. Add 1 tablespoon of oil and when hot add heaped dessertspoonfuls of the mixture. After a minute or so, once they have begun to form a crust, flatten each patty down a little with the spatula. Cook for around 2–3 minutes, until golden brown. Turn over and cook for a few minutes on the other side, until also golden. You may need to do this in batches, depending on the size of your pan.

Serve immediately, with the citrus chilli oil, soy, or the soy, honey and vinegar mix.

For the citrus chilli oil

1 tbsp crispy chilli oil, mostly the bits (see page 16)

1 tsp rice vinegar

1 tsp light soy sauce

zest of 1 clementine or orange

1 tbsp clementine or orange juice (eat the rest!)

For the udon gyoza

1 pack of ready-to-wok udon noodles (150g)

100g beef mince

2 tsp light soy sauce

2 cloves of garlic, crushed

2 tsp grated fresh ginger (approx. 4cm)

1 spring onion, finely sliced

1 egg

1 tbsp cornflour

neutral oil, to fry

To serve (optional)

citrus chilli oil

or light soy sauce

or 2 tsp each of light soy sauce, honey and rice vinegar

salads

Thai Prawn & Grapefruit Salad with Citrussy Dressing

Serves: 2–4

Prep: 15 mins

Cook: 5 mins

For the dressing

2 tbsp fish sauce

2½ tbsp soft brown sugar

2 tbsp tamarind paste (see pages 20–21)

2 tbsp clementine juice (or orange juice if none available)

3 tbsp fresh lime juice (approx. 2 limes)

1–2 red chillies, finely chopped (bird's-eye if you like it spicy, otherwise mild)

For the salad

300g Chinese leaf or Napa cabbage, shredded (approx. ½ a medium cabbage)

200g cooked king prawns

1 pink (or red) grapefruit, peeled and cut into bite-size pieces

a handful of fresh mint leaves, shredded

a handful of fresh coriander leaves

3 tbsp salted peanuts, roughly chopped

3 tbsp shop-bought crispy onions

Such is my and my husband's love of chillies, we decided to name each table at our wedding after a different one. We had Bird's Eye, Scotch Bonnet, Dutch Red – the list went on! We chose a spicy Thai prawn and grapefruit salad as our starter, inspired by yum som o – a Thai pomelo salad, often served with prawns. I couldn't not include a recipe for it, so here is my take on that original. With a caramelized dressing for extra depth, clementine juice for tangy sweetness, juicy prawns and plenty of crunch, this lively, zingy salad is everything I want Thai food to be and more.

Place the fish sauce, sugar and tamarind paste in a small saucepan and combine. Bring to a simmer over a medium heat, then reduce the heat slightly and bubble for a couple of minutes or so until it becomes syrupy. Take off the heat and leave to cool while you prepare the salad ingredients.

Once cool, add the clementine and lime juices, along with the chillies, and stir to combine.

Put the cabbage, prawns, grapefruit, mint and coriander leaves into a large mixing bowl. Pour over the dressing and toss to coat. Tip on to a serving platter or divide between 2–4 dishes. Scatter over the peanuts and crispy onions and serve immediately.

TIP: Make the dressing before you prepare the salad ingredients. This will give it time to cool.

TIP: Grapefruits can vary in sweetness and bitterness. If yours is particularly bitter, you may wish to add 1–2 teaspoons of extra sugar to the dressing.

Kimchi Caesar Salad

Serves:	Prep:	Cook:
2	15 mins	10 mins

For the salad

1 thick slice of sourdough
   (approx. 50g)
1 clove of garlic
1 tbsp neutral oil
sea salt flakes
2 large eggs, room
   temperature
1 romaine lettuce, cut into
   bite-size pieces
1 tbsp toasted sesame seeds
   (optional)

For the dressing

4 tbsp mayo
2 tsp rice vinegar
2 tsp gochujang
10g Parmesan
100g kimchi, chopped

All the creaminess and crunch of a Caesar salad – but with an Asian twist. Adding kimchi to the mayo dressing brings a spicy tang to the salad, while gochujang lends sweet heat and depth of flavour. The combination with crisp lettuce, golden croutons, salty Parmesan and a jammy egg works unbelievably well.

Preheat the oven to 200°C/180°C fan/gas mark 6. Put the kettle on for the eggs.

Rub the sourdough with the garlic, then cut or tear into 2cm chunks. Place in a baking tray with 1 tablespoon of oil and a pinch of salt, and combine well. Bake for 8–10 minutes, or until the croutons are golden and crispy.

Meanwhile, fill a small pan with the boiled water and bring to a rolling boil. Add the eggs and set the timer for 6½–7 minutes, depending on how done you like your eggs. Remove them from the pan and place in cold water. Once cool, peel the eggs and cut into quarters.

In a mixing bowl, combine the ingredients for the dressing. Tip in the lettuce along with half the croutons, and toss to coat.

Divide the lettuce between two plates. Top with the remaining croutons, followed by the egg and sesame seeds, if using. Serve immediately.

TIP Romaine lettuce is also known as cos lettuce. If you can't get hold of it, use two little gems instead.

SWITCH Why not add some cooked prawns or chicken for variety?

Charred Lettuce with Miso Mayo & Salty Crumbs

| Serves: 2 | Prep: 5 mins | Cook: 10 mins |

½ a small red onion, thinly sliced

2 tbsp rice vinegar

sea salt flakes

1 corn on the cob, kernels removed

neutral oil, to fry

2 tbsp panko breadcrumbs (or other fine breadcrumbs)

1 anchovy fillet or 1 tsp capers, chopped

2 little gem lettuces, quartered with the stem intact

For the dressing

1 tsp white miso paste

1 tbsp water

2 tbsp mayo

1 small clove of garlic, crushed

1 tsp rice vinegar

As with so many vegetables, charring transforms lettuce into something on a completely different level, making it sweet, nutty and smoky. What I love about this salad are the layers of flavour and texture – think creamy, garlicky dressing, salty, crispy crumbs, vinegar-spiked onions and sweet corn. What a combination!

Place the red onion, vinegar and a pinch of salt in a small bowl and combine. Set aside.

Combine the miso paste and water in another small bowl, then whisk in the remaining dressing ingredients. It should be a thick drizzling consistency. Add 1 teaspoon of water at a time if you need to thin it out. Set aside.

Heat a frying pan over a high heat and add the corn kernels. Cook for 2–3 minutes, turning occasionally, until starting to char. Remove from the pan.

Reduce the heat slightly and drizzle a little oil into the frying pan. Add the breadcrumbs and anchovies or capers, and fry for 1–2 minutes until golden, stirring constantly. If using anchovies, use a wooden spoon to break them down. Transfer to a bowl and return the frying pan to a high heat.

Brush a little oil on each lettuce wedge, along with a pinch of salt. Add the lettuce to the pan, cut side down. Cook for 1–2 minutes on each cut side, until charred.

Place half the corn on a serving plate and top with the lettuce. Drizzle over the dressing, then scatter over the pickled red onions, the rest of the corn and a good dusting of the salty crumbs. Serve immediately.

Spicy Smoked Mackerel Salad with Bagel Croutons

Serves:
2

Prep:
10 mins

Cook:
10 mins

½ a bagel, cut into
  2cm cubes
1 tbsp neutral oil
sea salt flakes
60g watercress and/or
  rocket leaves
1 carrot, julienned
5 radishes, thinly sliced
¼ of a cucumber, thinly
  sliced
100g smoked mackerel,
  skinned and flaked

For the dressing
2 tsp gochujang
2 tsp light soy sauce
2 tsp rice vinegar
2 tsp honey
2 tbsp natural yoghurt

This recipe is one of my new favourite ways of enjoying smoked mackerel. It takes less than 20 minutes to prepare, and the combination of creamy spicy dressing, crunchy bagel croutons, peppery radishes, cucumber and carrot is just sublime!

Preheat the oven to 220°C/200°C fan/gas mark 7.

Place the bagel pieces in a roasting tray, drizzle over the oil, add a good pinch of salt, and place in the oven for 7 minutes or so, until golden and toasted.

Meanwhile, combine all the ingredients for the dressing in a small bowl and set aside.

Once the croutons are ready, assemble the dish. Place all the ingredients for the salad, apart from the croutons, in a large bowl and pour over half the dressing. Combine.

Place on a serving platter and top with the croutons. Drizzle over the remaining dressing and serve immediately.

VEGAN | Swap the smoked mackerel for roast veg such as courgettes, aubergines or red peppers; the honey for agave; and the yoghurt for a dairy-free version.

Sticky Roast Parsnip & Chickpea Salad

Serves: 4

Prep: 15 mins

Cook: 30–35 mins

500g parsnips, peeled and cut into thick batons

3 tbsp neutral oil

sea salt flakes

1 x 400g tin of chickpeas, drained and dried with kitchen paper

For the dressing/glaze

3 tbsp gochujang

2 tbsp honey

2 tbsp rice vinegar

2 tbsp neutral oil

2 tbsp lime juice (approx. 1½ limes)

2 tsp water

For the salad

4 tbsp mixed seeds

150g mixed salad leaves

½ a cucumber, thinly sliced

1 apple, thinly sliced

80g Stilton cheese or feta

I love a roasted parsnip, all gnarly, crispy and gorgeously caramelized. In this recipe, their natural sweetness is elevated with the sweet and spicy gochujang glaze, which also doubles up as a dressing. Roasted chickpeas and toasted seeds add crunch, the cheese adds a creamy tang, while mixed leaves, cucumber and apple give a lovely freshness. A fabulous, action-packed salad.

Preheat the oven to 220°C/200°C fan/gas mark 7.

Place the parsnips on a large roasting tray. Drizzle over 2 table-spoons of oil, along with a good pinch of salt, and toss to coat.

Roast for 10 minutes, then remove from the oven. Move the parsnips to one side and tip in the chickpeas. Drizzle the chickpeas with 1 tablespoon of oil, then add a pinch of salt and toss to coat. Return to the oven for a further 25 minutes or until the parsnips are cooked through and caramelized, turning them halfway (give the chickpeas a stir at the same time).

Meanwhile, make the dressing and glaze. Whisk together the gochujang, honey and rice vinegar. This is your base glaze. Place half in another bowl and whisk in the oil, lime and water. This is your dressing.

To toast your seeds, place a small frying pan over a medium heat. Add the seeds and cook for a few minutes, stirring frequently, until they begin to pop and become toasted.

Remove the roasting tray from the oven and pour over the glaze. Combine well.

To assemble, mix the salad leaves, cucumber and apple with half the dressing. Place on a serving plate and add the parsnips and chickpeas. Spoon over a little more dressing and top with the crumbled cheese and toasted seeds. Serve immediately with the remaining dressing on the side. Any leftover dressing can be stored in the fridge.

Vietnamese Rice Noodle Salad with Halloumi

Serves:	Prep:	Cook:
2	15 mins	5 mins

For the carrot pickle
1 carrot, julienned
3 tbsp rice vinegar
½ tsp sugar
a pinch of salt

For the dressing
2 tbsp fish sauce
1 small clove of garlic, crushed
1 red chilli, finely chopped (deseed if you prefer a milder heat)
2 tbsp lime juice (approx. 1½ limes)
1 tbsp rice vinegar
2 tsp sugar
1 tsp water

For the salad
100g vermicelli rice noodles
neutral oil, to fry
125g halloumi, cut into slices
1 tbsp sweet chilli sauce
a handful of fresh mint leaves
a handful of fresh coriander leaves
1 little gem lettuce
2 tbsp salted peanuts, chopped
1 lime, cut into wedges

When I'm craving something light yet zingy and full of flavour, my taste buds often lead me here. Inspired by the classic Vietnamese salad bún chả, which features rice noodles and pork, this recipe instead uses halloumi as the main element. Halloumi's irresistible saltiness works beautifully alongside the fragrant herbs, sweet, spicy dressing, crunchy peanuts and crisp lettuce.

Combine the ingredients for the carrot pickle in a bowl and set aside.

Cook the noodles according to the packet instructions, then drain and rinse. Set aside.

Combine the ingredients for the dressing in a small bowl. Taste and add any extra fish sauce, lime or sugar as needed. Set aside.

Heat a non-stick frying pan over a high heat and add a drizzle of oil. When hot, add the halloumi and cook for 1 minute or so on each side, until golden. Turn off the heat, then drizzle over the sweet chilli sauce and coat.

To serve, divide the noodles, herbs, lettuce, carrot pickle and halloumi between two plates. Pour the dressing over the noodles and salad. Scatter over the peanuts and serve with wedges of lime.

VEGAN Use soy instead of fish sauce, and crispy fried tofu (see page 98) instead of halloumi.

Miso Maple Roast Sweet Potato Salad

Serves: 4

Prep: 10 mins

Cook: 30 mins

For the salad

2 tbsp neutral oil

1 tbsp maple syrup

2 tsp white miso paste

600g sweet potatoes, skin on, cut into 2–3cm chunks

sea salt flakes

freshly ground black pepper

50g walnuts

3–4 little gem lettuces (depending on the size)

100g feta, broken into small pieces

For the dressing

2 tsp grated fresh ginger (approx. 4cm)

2 tsp white miso paste

2 tbsp maple syrup

4 tbsp rice vinegar

1 tsp sesame oil

2 tbsp neutral oil

sea salt flakes

Sweet potatoes are a great storecupboard ingredient. In this salad, they are tossed in a miso maple glaze before cooking, which brings out their natural sweetness and lends an umami note to the dish. I just love the zingy, vibrant ginger dressing, especially when you throw a sprinkling of tangy, salty feta into the mix!

Preheat the oven to 220°C/200°C fan/gas mark 7.

Whisk together the oil, maple syrup and miso. Place the sweet potatoes in a large roasting tray, then pour over the miso mixture and toss to coat. Sprinkle with a pinch of salt and a twist of pepper, and place in the oven for 25–30 minutes, until caramelized and cooked through, turning once.

While the potatoes are cooking, whisk together all the ingredients for the dressing with a pinch of salt and set aside.

Place the walnuts in a frying pan over a medium-high heat. Toast for a few minutes, turning frequently, until they start to colour. Roughly chop them and set aside.

Place the lettuce on a serving plate. Add the sweet potatoes and drizzle over half the dressing. Combine, then top with the feta, walnuts and the remaining dressing. Serve immediately.

Thai Pork with Zingy Orange & Apple Slaw

Serves:
4

Prep:
25 mins

Cook:
10 mins

For the pork

1 tbsp oyster sauce

1 tbsp fresh coriander stalks, finely chopped

¼ tsp freshly ground black pepper

4 cloves of garlic, crushed

1 tsp fish sauce

500g pork shoulder steaks (approx. 3 steaks)

1 tbsp neutral oil

For the dressing

2 tbsp orange juice (blood orange if available)

2 tbsp fish sauce

2 tbsp lime juice (approx. 1½ limes)

2 tbsp soft brown sugar

2 bird's-eye chillies, finely chopped (deseeded for a milder heat and/or use a mild chilli instead)

For the slaw

250g white cabbage, finely shredded

1 apple, cut into thin matchsticks

½ a small red onion, finely sliced

a large handful of fresh coriander leaves

a large handful of fresh mint leaves, shredded

This is my spin on Thai pork neck salad – yam moo yang. Here I've opted for pork shoulder steaks, which are more readily available in UK supermarkets and have the added bonus of cooking quickly as well. What really pulls the whole plate together is the slaw – a perfect balance of zingy, sweet, tart and spicy. The result is a fresh and feisty salad, packed with herbs and topped with juicy pork, that I could happily eat every day. I like to marinate the pork for as long as possible, so make sure to do that before you prep anything else for the dish.

Place the ingredients for the pork, apart from the pork steaks and oil, in a dish and combine. Add the pork and coat well. Leave to marinate while you prepare the rest of the ingredients.

Combine the ingredients for the dressing in a small bowl. Place the cabbage, apple and onion in a large bowl and set aside.

Heat 1 tablespoon of oil in a large non-stick frying pan over a medium-high heat. When hot, add the pork steaks and cook for 3–4 minutes on each side (depending on thickness), or until cooked through but still juicy. Leave to rest for a few minutes, then slice thinly.

Just before serving, pour the dressing over the slaw and combine. Add the coriander and mint and gently mix through. Place on a serving plate and top with the pork, along with any of the resting juices.

TIP If your coriander doesn't come with much of the stalk, use a mixture of leaves and stalks instead.

curries

Hoisin Keema Curry

Serves:
4

Prep:
5 mins

Cook:
25 mins

1 tbsp neutral oil
1 onion, finely chopped
sea salt flakes
3 cloves of garlic, crushed
1 tbsp grated fresh ginger
(approx. 6cm)
2 tbsp curry powder
(whichever heat preferred)
500g beef mince
1 x 400g tin of tomatoes
200ml chicken or beef stock
(use it to rinse out the tin
of tomatoes)
4 tbsp hoisin sauce
120g peas (I use frozen)
freshly ground black pepper

To serve
rice
coriander leaves
sliced chilli (optional)
yoghurt (optional)

This is the curry you make when you're tired or short of time and want something that requires little brain power, but that still makes your taste buds jump up and down. In this non-traditional take on an Indian keema curry, two of my staples, hoisin sauce and curry powder, become best friends to create a dish which does just that. So easy, so tasty!

Heat the oil in a large frying pan over a medium heat. Fry the onions, along with a good pinch of salt, for 3 minutes until starting to soften, stirring occasionally.

Add the garlic and ginger and fry for 1 minute, then add the curry powder and stir-fry for a further minute.

Turn the heat up to medium-high and add the beef mince. Cook for 3–4 minutes, until browned, breaking it up as you go. Add the tinned tomatoes, stock and hoisin. Combine, then reduce the heat to medium and simmer for around 15 minutes, stirring occasionally.

Stir in the peas a couple of minutes before the end of the cooking time, making sure they are hot before serving. Taste, and if necessary add a spoonful more of hoisin along with some salt and pepper.

Delicious served with rice, coriander leaves, fresh chilli and yoghurt.

T
I
P

Hoisin sauces can vary in terms of flavour and saltiness. Be sure to taste at the end and add any extra if necessary.

Southern Thai Beef Curry

Serves: 2

Prep: 5 mins

Cook: 10 mins

1 tbsp neutral oil

1 tbsp Thai red curry paste (see tip)

½ tsp freshly ground black pepper

¼ tsp ground turmeric

¼ tsp ground cumin

¼ tsp ground coriander

1 x 200g sirloin steak, thinly sliced

200ml coconut milk

1 tsp fish sauce

1 tsp sugar

100g sugar snap peas

To serve

rice

Good-quality shop-bought Thai red curry paste is one of my absolute essentials, and forms the basis of many of my recipes, including this dish. The addition of ground turmeric, coriander and cumin, commonly used in southern Thai cuisine, adds complexity and depth of flavour to the curry. Super-speedy, rich and completely delicious.

Put 1 tablespoon of oil into a large deep frying pan over a medium heat. When the oil is hot, add the curry paste and fry for 1 minute or so, until fragrant, then add the pepper, turmeric, cumin and coriander and stir-fry for a further 30–60 seconds.

Add the steak and coat it in the paste, then add the coconut milk, fish sauce and sugar.

Tip in the sugar snap peas and simmer for 2–3 minutes, or until the beef and the sugar snap peas are just cooked. Taste and add any extra sugar or fish sauce if needed.

Serve with rice.

TIP I use Mae Ploy curry paste, which is spicier and more pungent than many others. If using a different brand you may need to add more paste and seasoning.

SWITCH Feel free to use whatever veg you have – green beans, mangetout, red peppers and baby corn all work well.

Aromatic Coconut Salmon Curry

Serves:
4

Prep:
15 mins

Cook:
25 mins

1 tbsp neutral oil

1 onion, finely chopped

sea salt flakes

2 cloves of garlic, finely chopped

1 tbsp grated fresh ginger (approx. 6cm)

½ tsp Chinese 5-spice

1 tbsp curry powder (whichever heat preferred)

1 tsp chilli flakes (optional)

1 medium tomato, chopped

1 x 400ml tin of coconut milk

150ml water

2 tbsp light soy sauce

2 tsp sugar

4 x skinless salmon fillets (approx. 500g), cut into 3cm pieces

250g asparagus, cut into 3–4cm pieces

To serve

rice and/or flatbreads

fresh coriander leaves

Delicious with

Shanghai Spring Onion Flatbread (page 186)

In this dish, the oiliness of salmon is balanced perfectly against the aromatic curry sauce, which uses Chinese 5-spice as well as curry powder. This is a saucy curry, so make sure you have rice and/or flatbreads to mop up all the deliciousness.

Heat 1 tablespoon of oil in a large deep frying pan over a medium heat. Add the onion with a pinch of salt, and cook for 3 minutes, stirring occasionally. Add the garlic and ginger, and stir-fry for a further 2–3 minutes, until softened.

Add the Chinese 5-spice, curry powder and chilli flakes, and fry for a further minute, adding another drizzle of oil if necessary.

Tip in the tomato along with the coconut milk, water, soy and sugar. Turn the heat up to medium high and bring to the boil. Bubble for 5 minutes, until the sauce thickens slightly, then taste the sauce and add any extra soy, salt or sugar as needed.

Add the salmon and coat it in the sauce. Reduce the heat to medium and cook for 3 minutes, stirring and turning over the salmon pieces occasionally. Add the asparagus and also coat in the sauce, being careful not to break up the salmon. Simmer for a further 2–3 minutes or so, until the salmon and asparagus are both cooked.

Serve with rice and/or flatbreads and sprinkled with coriander leaves.

 TIP If your asparagus is on the thick side, add it 1 minute earlier.

 VEGAN Swap the salmon for sweet potatoes or chickpeas.

Fragrant Butternut Squash & Black Bean Curry

Serves:	Prep:	Cook:
4	20 mins	35–40 mins

neutral oil, to fry

1 onion, finely sliced

1 tsp sea salt flakes

4 cloves of garlic, finely chopped

1 tbsp grated fresh ginger (approx. 6cm)

1 red chilli, finely chopped (deseed for a milder taste)

2 tbsp curry powder (whichever heat preferred)

½ tsp chilli flakes

1 x 400ml tin of coconut milk

400ml veg or chicken stock

1 medium butternut squash (approx. 1kg unpeeled weight, 750/800g prepared weight), peeled and cut into 2cm chunks

2 medium tomatoes, cut into wedges

1 tbsp tamarind paste (see pages 20–21)

1 tsp sugar

1 x 400g tin of black beans, drained

100g mangetout

To serve (optional)
fresh coriander leaves
red chilli, sliced
rice and/or flatbreads

This feel-good curry satisfies my takeaway cravings when I also want something nourishing and packed with veg. The butternut squash is delicately sweet and nutty, while being robust enough to carry the aromatic sauce. Black beans add texture along with the crunchy mangetout. A bowl of comforting goodness!

Heat 1 tablespoon of oil in a casserole dish or large saucepan over a medium heat. Add the onion and salt, and fry for around 5 minutes, stirring occasionally, until starting to soften. Add the garlic, ginger and fresh chilli and fry for another minute. Add the curry powder and chilli flakes and stir-fry for a further minute.

Stir in the coconut milk, stock, butternut squash, tomatoes, tamarind paste and sugar. Cover the pan, then turn the heat up to high and bring to the boil. Reduce the heat to a simmer and add the black beans. Cover again, but move the lid to one side, leaving a gap for steam to escape. Cook for 15 minutes, or until the squash is tender, stirring occasionally.

Add the mangetout, stir to combine, and simmer uncovered for 2–3 minutes, until just cooked. Taste and add any extra salt or sugar as needed. Scatter with coriander leaves and sliced red chillies, if using, and serve with rice and/or flatbreads.

 TIP Speed it up. Buy pre-prepared squash and save 10 minutes on the prep time. Alternatively, use sweet potato, which is quicker to prepare and cook.

 SWITCH Swap the black beans for chickpeas, and the mangetout for green beans or spinach.

Thai Red Celeriac Traybake Curry

Serves: 4

Prep: 10–15 mins

Cook: 50 mins

1 celeriac, peeled and cut into 2cm cubes

1 tbsp curry powder (whichever heat preferred)

sea salt flakes

2 tbsp neutral oil

2 tbsp Thai red curry paste (see tip)

200ml water

2 tsp fish sauce or light soy sauce

1 tsp sugar

1 x 400ml tin of coconut milk

100g kale

75g cashews, toasted

To serve

rice

wedges of lime

Celeriac can be quite intimidating, but once peeled and prepped, it becomes a versatile vegetable that can be roasted, mashed, used in soups and stews and even raw in salads and slaws. It has a delicate celery-like flavour and aroma. Roasting makes it slightly caramelized and brings out its sweet nuttiness, which works incredibly well in this fragrant Thai red curry. A light and healthy dish, with bold flavours.

Preheat the oven to 200°C/180°C fan/gas mark 6.

Place the celeriac in a large roasting tin. Sprinkle over the curry powder and a pinch of salt, then drizzle over the oil. Toss to coat. Roast for 30 minutes, or until tender.

Meanwhile, mix the curry paste with the water, then add the fish sauce and sugar.

Remove the celeriac from the oven and add the coconut milk and the red curry paste mixture. Don't worry if the coconut milk appears lumpy – it will melt once it is heated. Stir, then put back into the oven for a further 15 minutes.

Remove from the oven and mix in the kale, ensuring it is submerged where possible. Put back in the oven for a further 5 minutes, or until the kale is cooked. Taste the sauce and add any extra sugar, fish sauce/soy as needed. Stir in the cashews and serve with rice and wedges of lime.

T
I
P
I use Mae Ploy curry paste, which is spicier and more pungent than many others. If using a different brand, you may need to add more paste and seasoning.

T
I
P
Use a large sharp knife to cut the top and bottom off the celeriac, then peel it using a vegetable peeler.

Fiery Southern Thai Dry Pork Curry

Serves: 3–4

Prep: 5 mins

Cook: 10 mins

neutral oil

2 tbsp Thai red curry paste (see tip)

1 tsp ground turmeric

1 tsp ground cumin

1 tsp ground coriander

1–2 tsp red chilli flakes (reduce or omit if you prefer a milder heat)

500g pork mince (ideally 10% or more in fat)

100g green beans, halved if large

2 tsp fish sauce

1 tsp sugar

50ml water

zest of 1 lime

To serve

rice

wedges of lime

chopped fresh coriander

red chillies, sliced (optional)

Delicious with

Tangy Pickled Cabbage (page 188)

My auntie Dang used to love exploring London's Chinatown, and would often come back with a sachet of khua kling curry paste – a dry southern Thai curry known for its intense heat (a khua kling curry might typically use 20 bird's-eye chillies in the paste!). This recipe takes inspiration from that dish, using more widely available Thai red curry paste along with ground turmeric, cumin, coriander and lime zest. Although not as blow-your-head-off hot as the original, this version still packs a punch.

Heat 2 tablespoons of oil in a large frying pan or wok over a medium heat. Add the curry paste and stir-fry for 30–60 seconds or so, until fragrant and starting to change colour.

Add the turmeric, cumin, coriander and chilli flakes, and stir-fry for a few more seconds. Drizzle in a little more oil and turn up the heat to medium-high. Add the pork and stir-fry for a few minutes until cooked, breaking up the meat as you go. Make sure the pork is completely coated in the paste.

Add the green beans, fish sauce, sugar and water. Stir-fry for 2 or 3 minutes, until the beans are just cooked, adding a splash of water if necessary. Grate over the lime zest. Taste and add any extra fish sauce or sugar as necessary.

Serve with rice, wedges of lime, chopped coriander, and sliced red chilli, if you like it hot!

TIP: If using a lower-fat mince keep the heat on medium and add 1 tablespoon of oil to prevent it from drying out. You may also need to add an extra splash of water if necessary.

TIP: I use May Ploy curry paste, which is spicer and more pungent than many others. If using a different brand, you may need to add more paste and seasoning.

Malaysian Chicken, Chickpea & Spinach Curry

Serves: 4   Prep: 15 mins   Cook: 30 mins

neutral oil, to fry

1 large onion, finely chopped

¼ tsp sea salt flakes

4 cloves of garlic, finely chopped

1 tbsp grated fresh ginger (approx. 6cm)

2 tbsp curry powder (whichever heat preferred)

1 tbsp ground turmeric

6 skinless, boneless chicken thighs (approx. 450–500g), cut into 3cm pieces

2 medium tomatoes, chopped

1 x 400ml tin of coconut milk

1 x 400g tin of chickpeas, drained

1 tbsp light soy sauce

2 tsp sugar

freshly ground black pepper, to taste

100g spinach

To serve

fresh coriander leaves

rice and/or flatbreads

Delicious with

Shanghai Spring Onion Flatbread (page 186)

A gorgeous aromatic curry, ideal for that midweek curry fix. This recipe uses skinless, boneless chicken thighs, which not only retain their moisture but cook quickly, as well as that storecupboard favourite and best friend of curries – chickpeas! With added spinach for greenery, this is a hearty and satisfying dish – and one of my children's most requested!

Heat 2 tablespoons of oil in a large saucepan over a medium heat. Fry the onion with the salt for 5–7 minutes, until softened, stirring occasionally. Add the garlic and ginger and reduce the heat slightly. Cook for another couple of minutes, stirring often to prevent it burning. You may need to add another drizzle of oil.

Add the curry powder and turmeric, along with a little more oil if necessary. Stir-fry for another minute. Add the chicken and coat in the spicy onion mix. Cook for a few minutes until sealed, stirring frequently.

Add the tomatoes, coconut milk, chickpeas, soy and sugar. Increase the heat and bring to the boil. Lower the heat slightly and bubble for 10 minutes, until the chicken is cooked through and the sauce thickened slightly. Taste the sauce and add any pepper or extra salt, sugar or soy if needed.

Stir through the spinach and once wilted turn off the heat. Scatter over the coriander leaves and serve with rice and/or flatbreads.

noodles

Chiang Mai Curried Noodles with Crispy Coconut Tofu

Serves:
2

Prep:
15 mins

Cook:
25 mins

This dish, my take on Chiang Mai curried noodles – also known as khao soi – uses Thai red curry paste, and while not completely authentic is still sensational. This recipe heroes tofu – dipped in sweet chilli and coated in coconut, the crispy, nutty nuggets are pure deliciousness.

For the noodle soup

2 portions of medium egg noodles

neutral oil, to fry

175g chestnut mushrooms, sliced

2 tsp Thai red curry paste (see tip)

2 tsp curry powder (whichever heat preferred)

½ tsp ground turmeric

1 x 400ml tin of coconut milk

200ml chicken or veg stock

2 tsp light soy sauce

1 tsp sugar, or to taste

For the tofu

4 tbsp desiccated coconut

4 tbsp panko breadcrumbs

fine salt

3 tbsp sweet chilli sauce

150g extra firm tofu, patted dry and cut into bite-size cubes

2 tbsp plain flour

To serve (optional)

fresh coriander leaves

lime wedges

sliced red chillies

¼ of a small red onion or 1 spring onion, thinly sliced

sliced gherkins/cornichons or Tangy Pickled Cabbage (page 188)

Cook the noodles according to the packet instructions, then drain.

Meanwhile, take three bowls. Mix together the desiccated coconut and panko breadcrumbs in one bowl, with a pinch of salt. Put the sweet chilli sauce into the second bowl and the tofu into the third.

Sprinkle the flour over the tofu to coat. Add the tofu to the sweet chilli sauce, leaving behind any excess flour, and coat. Finally, place the tofu in the coconut and panko mix and coat well. Set aside.

Put 1 tablespoon of oil into a pan over a medium heat. When hot, add the mushrooms with a pinch of salt. Cook for 2 minutes, until starting to soften. Add the curry paste, curry powder and turmeric along with a drizzle more oil, and stir-fry for a further minute or so.

Pour in the coconut milk, stock, soy and sugar, and turn up the heat. Bring to the boil, then reduce the heat slightly and simmer for 5 minutes. Taste and add any extra soy or sugar as needed.

Meanwhile, cook the tofu. Heat 2 tablespoons of oil in a large non-stick frying pan over a medium heat. When very hot, add the tofu, leaving behind any excess crumbs, and cook for 5–10 minutes, until golden all over. Leave untouched for the first minute or so, to help it develop a nice crust. Be careful not to let it burn.

Just before serving, pour a little boiling water over the noodles to warm them up, then divide the noodles between two bowls and ladle over the soup and mushrooms. Top with the tofu and add the coriander leaves, lime wedges, chillies, onion and gherkins or pickles, if using.

TIP

There are a few elements, so read through the recipe and have everything laid out and ready to go.

TIP

I use May Ploy curry paste, which is spicer and more pungent than many others. If using a different brand, you may need to add more paste and seasoning.

Sticky Orange Beef Noodles

Serves: 2

Prep: 15 mins

Cook: 15 mins

This is my take on the sweet and tangy Chinese dish, orange beef stir-fry. Usually made with beef and vegetables, I've added noodles to change things up. The glossy, fruity sauce laced with orange juice and zest brings it all together. Quick, tasty and on repeat!

For the stir-fry

1 x 250g sirloin steak, thinly sliced

1 tbsp cornflour

1 tbsp light soy sauce

2 portions of medium egg or wheat noodles

neutral oil, to fry

1 small onion, sliced

2 cloves of garlic, finely chopped

1 tsp grated fresh ginger (approx. 2cm)

1 red pepper, sliced

100g broccoli, cut into small bite-size florets

For the sauce

1 tsp cornflour

1 tbsp water

zest of 1 orange

100ml orange juice (approx. 1½–2 oranges)

3 tbsp light soy sauce

1 tbsp honey

1 tbsp sweet chilli sauce

1 tsp rice vinegar

½ tsp chilli flakes (optional)

sea salt flakes

To serve

1 spring onion, finely sliced

Place the steak in a dish and add 1 tablespoon of cornflour and the soy. Mix and leave to marinate while you prepare the rest of the ingredients.

Cook the noodles according to the packet instructions. Drain and rinse under cold water.

Meanwhile, make the sauce. Mix the cornflour and water together in a small bowl to form a paste, then add the rest of the sauce ingredients with a pinch of salt. Set near the stove.

Heat 1 tablespoon of oil in a large non-stick frying pan or wok over a high heat. When hot, add the beef, spreading it out in a thin layer. Fry for 1–2 minutes, until browned but not completely cooked through. Remove and set aside. Scrape off any burnt bits from the pan and discard.

Heat another 1 tablespoon of oil and add the onion, garlic and ginger. Stir-fry for a couple of minutes, then add the red pepper and broccoli. Stir-fry for 1 minute, then pour in the sauce and reduce the heat to medium-high. Bubble for 2 minutes or so, until thickened and the broccoli and pepper are tender-crisp, then tip in the noodles and beef.

Stir-fry for a minute or so, until the noodles are fully coated. Taste and if it needs a little more sweetness, add an extra teaspoon of honey. Serve immediately, garnished with spring onions.

Spicy Garlic & Ginger Lamb Noodles

Serves: 2 generously   **Prep:** 10 mins   **Cook:** 10 mins

For the stir-fry
150g flat rice noodles

1 tbsp neutral oil, to fry

2 spring onions, finely sliced

1 tbsp grated fresh ginger (approx. 6cm)

3 cloves of garlic, finely chopped

250g lamb mince (10% fat if possible)

150g spring greens, shredded, and/or pak choi, chopped into bite-size pieces

1 tsp rice vinegar

For the sauce
1 tbsp white miso paste

2 tbsp light soy sauce

2 tbsp honey

1 tbsp rice vinegar

1½ tbsp sriracha

1 tsp red chilli flakes

For the red chillies in vinegar (optional)
1–2 red chillies, finely sliced (according to taste)

3–4 tbsp rice vinegar or white wine vinegar

To serve
1 spring onion, finely sliced

red chillies in vinegar

This is the sort of dish that would cure a hangover. Rich, spicy, salty, sour and sweet – it hits your mouth from all sides. Taking centre stage is the unctuous, crisp-fried lamb mince, amplified by a punchy trio of garlic, ginger and fiery chilli. Soy and miso provide the umami factor, while honey adds sweetness.

Cook the noodles according to the packet instructions.

Meanwhile, whisk together the ingredients for the sauce and set near the stove.

Heat 1 tablespoon of oil in a large frying pan over a high heat. Once very hot, add the spring onions and stir-fry for 30 seconds or so. Add the ginger and garlic and fry for another few seconds.

Add the lamb and cook for around 5–7 minutes, until lovely and crispy in bits, breaking up the meat as you go. Don't stir too often, to allow the lamb to become golden.

While it is cooking, mix together the red chillies and vinegar, if using, in a small dish and set aside.

Pour the sauce into the pan and combine well. Add the greens and stir-fry for a minute or two, until they have almost wilted, then tip in the noodles. Stir-fry until the noodles are well coated, then take off the heat.

Drizzle over 1 teaspoon of vinegar and combine. Taste and add a dash of soy, honey or sriracha if necessary. Serve immediately, scattered with spring onions, with the red chillies in vinegar on the side.

 TIP It is important to have a very high heat when cooking the lamb, to help it go crispy.

 TIP Lamb can be a fatty meat. If your pan becomes too oily while cooking the mince, you may prefer to get rid of a little of the excess.

Kimchi Beef Peanut Butter Ramen

Serves:
2

Prep:
10 mins

Cook:
20 mins

For the steak
1 x 200–250g sirloin steak
1 tsp toasted sesame oil
1 tbsp light soy sauce

For the noodles
2 nests of medium egg/
  wheat noodles
4 tbsp unsweetened peanut
  butter
2 tbsp gochujang
1 tbsp light soy sauce
1 tbsp sugar
600ml chicken stock
neutral oil, to fry
2 spring onions, sliced
2 large eggs, room
  temperature
  if possible

To serve
100g kimchi, chopped
  (I use scissors)
1 spring onion, finely sliced

When I've had a busy day and I'm in the mood for comfort and some gentle chilli heat, this is exactly what I crave. The rich, nutty broth is thick and almost curry-like, and works so well with the soy-marinated beef, creamy soft-boiled eggs and kimchi – which gives pops of tanginess and crunch. A very satisfying, slurptastic dish!

Place the steak in a dish and coat with the sesame oil and 1 tablespoon of soy. Leave to marinate while you prepare the rest of the dish.

Cook the noodles according to packet instructions. Drain, rinse and set aside in the colander.

Meanwhile, whisk together the peanut butter, gochujang, soy and sugar with a little of the stock, adding it slowly until you have a smooth paste. Set aside.

Heat a drizzle of oil in a large saucepan over a medium heat. Add the spring onions and fry for a minute or so. Add the remaining stock along with the peanut butter mixture, and combine. Bring to the boil, then reduce the heat to the lowest setting and cover.

Bring a pan of water to the boil over a high heat. Reduce the heat to medium and add the eggs. Cook for 6½–7 minutes, depending on how soft you like your eggs. Place in cold water.

Meanwhile, heat a drizzle of oil in a frying pan over a high heat and when very hot, add the steak, leaving behind any excess marinade. Cook for 1–2 minutes each side, depending on how you like it done. Remove and leave to rest.

Peel and halve the eggs. Pour a little boiling water over the noodles to warm them, then divide between two bowls. Slice the steak thinly.

Ladle the broth over the noodles, and top with the beef and its resting juices, eggs, kimchi and spring onion. Serve immediately.

Portobello Noodle Traybake

Serves:
2

Prep:
10 mins

Cook:
15–20 mins

For the sauce
3 tbsp hoisin sauce
3 tbsp sriracha
2 tbsp rice wine vinegar

For the traybake
2 portions of medium ready-to-wok or fresh noodles, wheat or egg
½ a red pepper, thinly sliced
1 tbsp sesame oil
100g mangetout
50g cashew nuts
4 portobello mushrooms
2–3 tsp crispy chilli oil, a mix of bits and oil (see tip)
sea salt flakes

To serve
fresh coriander leaves and/or sliced spring onions
wedges of lime

My noodle traybakes are always a hit. With minimal hands-on time, this dish makes an ideal midweek meal that's full of flavour and texture. Pre-cooked noodles are coated in a sweet and spicy sauce and roasted until they become both sticky and crispy. Mangetout, peppers and cashews provide crunch, while the portobello mushrooms add a meaty richness. A light but satisfying meal.

Preheat the oven to 200°C/180°C fan/gas mark 6.

Combine the ingredients for the sauce, reserving 2 tablespoons for the final dish.

Place the noodles in a large oven tray and add the red pepper. Drizzle over the sesame oil and sauce, and combine well. Spread out into a thin layer and place in the oven for 5 minutes.

Remove the noodles from the oven and toss through the mangetout and cashews. Place the mushrooms on top. Drizzle chilli oil over each one, and add a small pinch of salt.

Place in the oven for 15 minutes, or until the mushrooms are cooked through and tender. Scatter over the coriander leaves and/or spring onions, and serve with wedges of lime and with the reserved sauce on the side.

 T I P If your chilli oil has more bits than oil you may need to drizzle over a little extra oil to moisten the mushrooms.

 T I P If you don't have chilli oil, see page 194, for making your own, or combine 1 tablespoon of oil with 2 small crushed garlic cloves, ¼–½ tsp of chilli flakes and a couple of pinches of salt.

Stir-fried Curry Noodles

Serves:
2

Prep:
10 mins

Cook:
10 mins

This is why I love my storecupboard. With just a few simple core ingredients you can whip up the most delicious of dinners in no time at all, including these street food-worthy Malaysian-inspired noodles. Curry powder, a common ingredient in Malaysian cooking, adds warmth and earthiness, while the sriracha adds a back note of heat. The soy, honey and ketchup add salt, sweetness and tang. Tasty, satisfying and easy!

For the stir-fry
2 portions of medium wheat or egg noodles
neutral oil, to fry
2 eggs, beaten
1 small onion, sliced
2 cloves of garlic, finely chopped
1 carrot, thinly sliced
½ a sweetheart/hispi cabbage, cut into 3cm pieces

For the sauce
1 tsp curry powder (whichever heat preferred)
3 tbsp light soy sauce
2 tbsp honey
1 tbsp sriracha
1 tbsp ketchup

To serve
wedges of lime
fresh coriander leaves
sliced red chillies (optional)
a handful of salted peanuts

Delicious with
Quick Radish Pickle with Garlic, Ginger & Chilli (page 191)

Cook the noodles according to the packet instructions.

Meanwhile, place the ingredients for the sauce in a small bowl and combine. Set near the stove.

Place 1 tablespoon of oil in a large frying pan or wok over a high heat. Add the eggs and lightly scramble until just set. Push to one side (if possible, moving that side of the pan slightly off the heat), and add another 1 tablespoon of oil. Tip in the onion, garlic, carrot and cabbage, and stir-fry for 2–3 minutes, until softened.

Add the noodles to the pan with the sauce. Combine well and stir-fry for another minute or so. Serve immediately, garnished with wedges of lime, coriander leaves, red chillies and peanuts.

TIP
If your frying pan or wok is on the smaller side you may wish to remove the eggs while you cook the veg, putting them back in with the noodles and sauce.

SWITCH
Would be great with some added prawns or chicken. Feel free to use whatever veg you have to hand, bearing in mind that cooking times may vary.

Chinese Crispy Noodle Cake with Stir-fried Veg

Serves: 2 **Prep:** 15 mins **Cook:** 20 mins

If, like me, you're a fan of 'the crispy bits' this is a dish for you! The noodles are fried in a cake shape until crispy and golden brown and served with a delicious saucy topping.

2 portions of medium egg or wheat noodles

1 tsp neutral oil, plus more to fry (see tip)

2 spring onions, cut into 4cm pieces

2 cloves of garlic, finely chopped

1 carrot, thinly sliced on the diagonal

100g chestnut mushrooms, thinly sliced

½ a green pepper, thinly sliced

For the sauce

1 tbsp cornflour

2 tbsp light soy sauce

2 tbsp mirin (or use 2 tbsp rice vinegar + 1 tsp sugar)

1 tbsp soft brown sugar

2 tsp white miso paste

½ tsp chilli flakes (optional)

175ml water

To serve

sliced spring onions

Preheat the oven to 170°C/150°C fan/gas mark 3.

Cook the noodles according to the packet instructions. Drain and rinse, then dry well with kitchen paper. Toss with 1 teaspoon of oil and set aside.

Meanwhile, put the cornflour into a small bowl, then add the soy to make a paste. Whisk in the remaining sauce ingredients apart from the water, making sure the miso dissolves. Once combined whisk in the water and set aside.

Heat a large non-stick frying pan over a medium-high heat. Add 1–2 tablespoons of oil and once hot tip in the noodles, spreading them out in a thin layer. Press down to make sure they have contact with the pan. Cook for 4–5 minutes, without touching, until crispy and golden on the bottom. Take a large ovenproof plate and carefully invert the noodles on to it. Add another 1–2 tablespoons of oil to the pan and slide the noodles back in, pressing down again. Cook for another 4–5 minutes, until the bottom is crispy. Slide the crispy noodles back on to the plate and place in the oven to keep warm.

Turn up the heat to high, then add 1 tablespoon of oil to the pan. Add the spring onions and fry for 30 seconds, then add the garlic and stir-fry for a few more seconds. Add the rest of the veg and stir-fry for a couple of minutes. Pour in the sauce and reduce the heat to medium. Bubble for a couple of minutes or so, until the sauce has thickened and the veg are just cooked.

To serve, cut the crispy noodle cake into wedges, then pile the stir-fried veg into the middle. Serve immediately, sprinkled with sliced spring onions.

T I P
For a healthier version use 1 tablespoon of oil to fry the noodles – it may not be quite as crispy but will still be delicious!

S W I T C H
If you have oyster sauce to hand, you can swap it for the mirin and white miso paste. Simply use 3 tablespoons of oyster sauce in their place, with just 1 tablespoon of soy instead of 2 tablespoons.

Prawn & Chorizo Sweet Soy Noodles

Serves:
2

Prep:
10 mins

Cook:
10 mins

For the sauce

3 tbsp oyster sauce

2 tbsp light soy sauce

1 tbsp honey

1 tsp ground coriander

For the stir-fry

150g flat rice noodles, wide if possible

neutral oil, to fry

50g chorizo ring, cut in half lengthways and sliced into half-moons

2 large eggs, beaten

2 spring onions, roughly chopped

2 cloves of garlic, finely chopped

100g spring greens, finely shredded

150g raw king prawns

To serve

1 spring onion, finely sliced

Loosely inspired by Char kway teow – a stir-fried noodle dish popular in Malaysia and Singapore – this dish uses chorizo instead of the more traditional Chinese sausage lap cheong. The crispy, salty morsels are like gems, adding intense flavour to every bite, while bringing out the delicacy of the prawns. Together with an umami-bursting sauce made of oyster sauce, soy and honey, this is just what I want from a plate of stir-fried noodles!

Cook the noodles according to packet instructions. Drain, rinse and set aside.

Meanwhile, mix together the ingredients for the sauce in a small bowl and set near the stove.

Heat a drizzle of oil in a large non-stick frying pan or wok. Add the chorizo and fry for a minute or two until browned. Remove with a slotted spoon.

Add 1 tablespoon of oil to the pan and pour in the eggs. Lightly scramble and when fluffy, push to the side (if possible, moving that side of the pan slightly off the heat). Add the spring onions and garlic and fry for 30 seconds, then add the spring greens. Cook for 1 minute or so, until starting to wilt. Push to the side and add the prawns. Stir-fry until they start to turn pink, then add the noodles, chorizo and sauce. Stir-fry for a couple of minutes until everything is well coated.

Serve immediately, sprinkled with the sliced spring onions.

T
I
P

Make sure you have all the elements ready by the stove before you start, as the dish cooks quickly.

Hot & Tangy Udon Noodles

Serves: 2

Prep: 10 mins

Cook: 15 mins

Hot, sweet and tangy, these satisfyingly chewy noodles hit the spot. It all comes down to the punchy sauce, made from four of my most used storecupboard ingredients – tamarind, soy, honey and sriracha. Although udon noodles are my favourite for this recipe, you can of course use whatever noodles you have in the cupboard.

For the sauce
3 tbsp tamarind paste (see pages 20–21)

2 tbsp honey

2½ tbsp light soy sauce

2 tbsp sriracha

For the stir-fry
neutral oil, to fry

150g extra firm tofu, patted dry and cut into bite-size cubes

1 carrot, cut into thin batons

150g pak choi, stalk cut into bite-size pieces, leaves cut lengthways

2 cloves of garlic, finely chopped

1 red chilli, finely chopped (deseed for a milder heat)

2 packets of ready-to-wok udon noodles

To serve
a handful of salted peanuts, roughly chopped

1 lime, cut into wedges (optional)

Combine the tamarind, honey, soy and sriracha in a small bowl and set near the stove.

Heat 1 tablespoon of oil in a large non-stick frying pan or wok over a medium-high heat. When the oil is very hot, add the tofu. Fry for around 5 minutes, or until golden all over, trying not to move it for the first minute or so. Remove from the pan.

Place another 1 tablespoon of oil in the pan and add the carrot. Stir-fry for 30 seconds, then tip in the pak choi stalks. Stir-fry for 1 minute, then add the garlic and chilli, and cook for another 30 seconds. Tip in the pak choi leaves and stir-fry until just wilted, then add the noodles along with the sauce. Reduce the heat to medium and stir-fry for 1 minute, or until the noodles are hot and everything is well combined.

Put the tofu back into the pan and toss to coat, making sure everything is thoroughly mixed. Turn off the heat and taste. Feel free to add another teaspoon of honey or a splash of soy if necessary. Serve immediately, sprinkled with chopped peanuts and wedges of lime, if using.

Use prawns or chicken instead of the tofu.

fish & prawns

Sticky Chilli Salmon

Serves: 2

Prep: 10 mins

Cook: 10–15 mins

For the sauce
2 tbsp ketchup
1½ tbsp light soy sauce
1 tbsp honey
2 tsp sriracha
1 clove of garlic, crushed
1 tsp rice wine or white wine vinegar
3 tbsp water

For the salmon
neutral oil, to fry
2 salmon fillets, cut into bite-size chunks
2 spring onions, cut into 3cm pieces

To serve
rice
1 spring onion, finely sliced

Delicious with
Chilli & Garlic Charred Broccoli (page 182)
Stir-fried Cabbage with Chilli Butter (page 180)

This dish is actually inspired by one of my most popular recipes from Dominique's Kitchen – my Sticky Chilli Chicken. Instead of chicken, we have salmon, cut into bite-size pieces, seared, then coated in a sticky, spicy, sweet sauce made from some of my storecupboard essentials – ketchup, soy, honey and sriracha. A different combination of ingredients from the original but just as delicious.

Combine the ingredients for the sauce in a small bowl and set aside.

Heat ½ tablespoon of oil in a large non-stick frying pan over a medium-high heat. When hot, add the salmon and fry for a couple of minutes or so, until seared on all sides. If the salmon has skin, cook until the skin side is crispy. Remove.

Heat another ½ tablespoon of oil and increase the heat to high. Add the spring onion pieces and stir-fry for about 30 seconds. Reduce the heat slightly and add the sauce. Bubble briefly, then put the salmon back into the pan. Simmer for a few minutes, until cooked, adding a splash of water if the sauce becomes too thick.

Serve with rice, topped with the finely sliced spring onions.

VEGAN Swap the salmon for crispy fried tofu (see page 98) or shiitake mushrooms, and the honey for agave syrup.

Chinese 5-spice Prawns

Serves:	Prep:	Cook:
4	10 mins	10 mins

This is the kind of dish that ticks all my boxes. Super-quick and easy, yet it has a depth of flavour thanks to the combination of aromatic Chinese 5-spice, soy, mirin and chilli oil. Honey adds a touch of sweetness to balance the savouriness and mild heat. A satisfying meal that always gets the thumbs-up!

For the sauce

1 tbsp cornflour

4 tbsp water

1½ tbsp honey

4 tbsp light soy sauce

2 tbsp mirin (or use 2 tbsp rice vinegar + 1 tsp sugar)

2 tbsp of crispy chilli oil, mostly the bits (see page 16)

2 tsp toasted sesame oil

½ tsp Chinese 5-spice

For the stir-fry

1 tbsp neutral oil

4 cloves of garlic, finely chopped

4 spring onions, sliced (greens reserved for garnish)

300g asparagus, cut into 4–5cm pieces

400g raw king prawns

To serve

rice

spring onion greens, sliced

Delicious with

Stir-fried Cabbage with Chilli Butter (page 180)

Pan-roasted Soy & Black Pepper Fennel (page 176)

Put the cornflour into a small bowl and gradually stir in the water to create a paste. Mix in the remaining ingredients for the sauce, and set near the stove.

Heat 1 tablespoon of oil in a large frying pan over a medium-high heat. Add the garlic and spring onions and stir-fry for 1 minute or so, until softened. Add the asparagus and cook for a couple of minutes. Turn up the heat, then add the prawns and stir-fry for 1 minute or so until they start to colour.

Add the sauce and stir-fry for a few moments until the prawns are cooked. If the sauce becomes too thick you may need to add another tablespoon of water.

Serve immediately with rice and garnish with the reserved spring onion greens.

S W I T C H Swap the prawns for chicken or pork fillet.

V E G A N Use crispy fried tofu (see page 98) instead of the prawns and agave instead of the honey.

Spiced Coconut Fish Traybake

Serves:
2

Prep:
5 mins

Cook:
25 mins

200g cherry tomatoes,
preferably on the vine

150g tenderstem broccoli

1 tbsp neutral oil

sea salt flakes

1 tbsp harissa paste

1 tsp grated fresh ginger
(approx. 2cm)

1 tsp fish sauce

1 tsp soft brown sugar

100ml coconut milk (see tip)

2 fillets of sustainable cod or
other white fish (approx.
250g), skinless

To serve
rice

*The secret to this recipe is the blend of harissa, ginger, fish sauce
and coconut milk. Harissa provides a concentrated flavour base
and a gentle smoky heat, while the ginger and fish sauce give
depth. Together with the coconut milk they create a fresh and
delicately spiced dish. Light, simple and perfect for midweek.*

Preheat the oven to 200°C/180°C fan/gas mark 6.

Place the tomatoes and broccoli in a large oven dish. Drizzle with
1 tablespoon of oil, add a good pinch of salt, and toss to coat.
Place in the oven for 10 minutes.

Meanwhile put the harissa, ginger, fish sauce, sugar and coconut
milk into a small bowl along with a pinch of salt, and combine.

Remove the tray from the oven and nestle the fish on top. Spoon
over the coconut mix and place in the oven for 10–15 minutes,
until the fish is cooked through. Serve with rice to mop up the juices.

T
I
P

Freeze your leftover
coconut milk.

Crispy Seabass with Tamarind & Tomato

Serves: 2

Prep: 15 mins

Cook: 25 mins

This is inspired by a dish I had on a visit to Burmese restaurant Lahpet in Covent Garden. Crisp, fried bream nestled on a bed of caramelized, jammy, tomatoey onions – the combination was completely delicious. This recipe is my home-style interpretation of that wonderful dish.

For the onions

1 tbsp neutral oil

2 medium onions, thinly sliced

sea salt flakes

3 cloves of garlic, finely chopped

1 tsp grated fresh ginger (approx. 2cm)

1 tbsp soft brown sugar

¼ tsp paprika

¼ tsp ground turmeric

¼–½ tsp chilli flakes, according to taste

125ml water

1 tbsp tomato purée

1 tbsp tamarind paste (see pages 20–21)

1 tsp light soy sauce

1 medium tomato, finely chopped

For the seabass

2 seabass fillets

¼ tsp ground turmeric

sea salt flakes

1 tbsp neutral oil

For the greens

100g spring greens or kale, shredded

To serve

salted peanuts, chopped

fresh coriander leaves

rice

Heat 1 tablespoon of oil in a large frying pan over a medium heat. Add the onions with a good pinch of salt, and fry for 5 minutes, until softened, stirring occasionally.

Meanwhile, dry the seabass with kitchen paper. Dust both sides of the fish with the ground turmeric and sprinkle the skin with salt. Set aside.

Add the garlic and ginger to the onions, and stir-fry for 1 minute or so, adding a drizzle of oil if necessary.

Add the sugar, paprika, turmeric and chilli flakes. Cook for a further 1 minute then add the water, tomato purée, tamarind, soy and tomato. Turn the heat down to medium-low and simmer for 3–5 minutes, until reduced and slightly jammy, stirring occasionally. Add any extra salt or sugar as needed.

Meanwhile, put the greens into a pan of salted boiling water and cook for 2–3 minutes, until just done but still bright green. Drain, tip back into the pan and cover to keep warm.

Heat 1 tablespoon of oil in a large non-stick frying pan over a medium-high heat. Once very hot, place the sea bass in the pan skin side down. Flatten each fillet with a spatula to ensure the skin has full contact with the pan.

Fry for 2½–3 minutes untouched, until the skin is golden and crispy, then turn over. Lower the heat to low/medium-low and cook for a further 1 minute or until cooked.

To serve, place the greens on a plate, spoon over the tomato sauce, then top with the seabass. Sprinkle with chopped nuts and coriander leaves. Delicious with rice.

One-pot Soy Butter Salmon

Serves: 2   Prep: 5 mins   Cook: 15 mins

1 onion, thinly sliced
1 medium leek, thinly sliced
100g chestnut mushrooms, thinly sliced
40g butter, cut into cubes
125ml water, wine or cooking sake
1½ tbsp light soy sauce
2 skinless salmon fillets

To serve
rice

This simple one-pot recipe was given to me by my Japanese friend and neighbour Misako Nishimura. One day, she gave me a bowl of this to sample. It was unassuming to look at, but I have to say I was taken aback by how good it was. A humble, mellow dish, it somehow delivers a gentle but wonderful umami-hit thanks to the soy/butter combination. With minimal prep, and completely hands-off once it goes on the stove, this is definitely a midweek winner.

Scatter the onions over the base of a large, deep, lidded frying pan. Layer over the leeks and then the mushrooms.

Dot the butter around the dish, then add the water and soy. Top with the salmon.

Place the lid on the pan and simmer over a medium heat for around 15 minutes, or until the salmon and mushrooms are cooked. You may need to lower the heat slightly if it bubbles too much.

Taste and add any extra soy. Serve with rice.

Tamarind Glazed Mackerel with Fennel Pickle

Serves:
2

Prep:
5 mins

Cook:
10 mins

For the pickled fennel
5 tbsp rice wine vinegar
½ tsp sugar
¼ tsp chilli flakes
1 small clove of garlic, crushed
a pinch of salt
½ a medium bulb of fennel (approx. 150g), thinly sliced

For the sauce
2 tbsp tamarind paste (see pages 20–21)
2 tbsp light soy sauce
2 tbsp honey
1 tbsp water

For the mackerel
2 mackerel fillets
sea salt flakes
neutral oil, to fry

To serve
rice

My Thai auntie Dang's tamarind sauce is now legendary. It not only served as the inspiration behind my tamarind, honey & sesame chicken – the dish that got me through the first round of The Great Cookbook Challenge TV show, but it also compelled me to start my sauce business, The Woolf's Kitchen. Here it makes another appearance in this light but flavour-packed dish. The sweet-sour tanginess of the tamarind works brilliantly with oily fish, as does the fennel, which cuts through and adds a refreshing touch.

Place the rice wine vinegar, sugar, chilli flakes, garlic and salt in a bowl and combine. Add the sliced fennel, combine well, and set aside.

Place all the ingredients for the sauce in a small pan on a medium heat. Bring to a simmer, then bubble for 2–3 minutes, until it has thickened and is slightly syrupy.

Pat the mackerel fillets dry and sprinkle a little sea salt over the skin. Heat a non-stick frying pan over a medium-high heat. Add a drizzle of oil, and when the pan is very hot, add the mackerel skin side down. Flatten with a spatula to prevent the fillets from curling up. Cook for 2–3 minutes, or until the skin is golden and crispy, then turn over. Lower the heat slightly and cook for another 30 seconds or so, until the flesh is just cooked. Remove from the pan.

Drizzle over the tamarind glaze and serve with the fennel pickle and some rice. Eat immediately.

SWITCH

Swap the mackerel for salmon and the fennel for white cabbage.

Chilli Tamarind Prawns with Mangetout

Serves: 2

Prep: 5 mins

Cook: 15 mins

For the sauce

1 tbsp tamarind paste (see pages 20–21)

1½ tsp oyster sauce

1 tsp light soy sauce

2 tbsp water

For the stir-fry

2 tbsp neutral oil

1 onion, finely chopped

sea salt flakes

4 cloves of garlic, crushed

1 tbsp soft brown sugar

½–1 tsp red chilli flakes

100g mangetout

200g raw king prawns

To serve

rice

Delicious with

Garlicky Soy Aubergines (page 170)

Tamarind & Honey Green Beans (page 178)

This recipe is my cheat's version of the Thai dish, goong pad nam prik pao – stir-fried prawns with chilli jam. Nam prik pao (the chilli jam part of the dish) is a quintessential part of Thai cuisine, but isn't always widely available. By caramelizing onions, garlic, sugar and chilli flakes along with tamarind, I've recreated the flavours in this spicy but sweet and garlicky stir-fry. Absolutely delicious and ready in no time at all.

Place the ingredients for the sauce in a small bowl and combine. Set near the stove.

Place 2 tablespoons of oil in a large frying pan or wok over a medium heat. Add the onion with a good pinch of salt and fry for around 5 minutes, until softened, stirring occasionally. Add the garlic and stir-fry for another couple of minutes. If it starts burning, lower the heat slightly.

Add the sugar and chilli flakes, and stir-fry for a further minute or 2, again being careful not to burn. Turn the heat up to high and add the mangetout. Stir-fry for 1 minute, then add the prawns. Stir-fry for another minute, or until the prawns have just started to turn pink, then add the sauce. Bubble for 1–2 minutes, until the prawns are cooked and the sauce has thickened slightly. Feel free to add another tablespoon or 2 of water if it becomes too dry.

Taste the sauce and add a pinch of salt, a splash of soy or sugar if needed. Serve immediately, with rice.

TIP If you have particularly big prawns, they may take longer. If so, feel free to add a splash of water to help prevent the sauce from drying out.

VEGAN Switch the prawns to crispy fried tofu (see page 98) and the oyster sauce to mushroom sauce/vegan oyster sauce or miso paste.

chicken

Thai Chicken Curry Pie

Serves:	Prep:	Cook:
6	10 mins	50 mins

neutral oil

1 leek, sliced

sea salt flakes

2 tbsp cornflour

2–3 tsp Thai red curry paste, according to preferred heat level (see tip)

2 tbsp curry powder (whichever heat preferred)

600g skinless, boneless chicken thighs, cut into 3cm pieces

250g chestnut mushrooms, sliced

1 x 400ml tin of coconut milk

2 tsp fish sauce

1 tsp soft brown sugar, optional

150g frozen peas

1 x 320g sheet of ready-made puff pastry (remove from the fridge just 10–15 minutes before use)

1 egg, beaten

To serve

mashed potatoes

yoghurt or sour cream (optional)

steamed green veg

Delicious with

Cumin & Chilli Roast Potatoes (page 174)

In this dish, the British classic chicken and mushroom pie gets a makeover. It has all the mellow comfort of the original but with added depth and a little spice. There is minimal prep, as most of the work is done in the oven, making it perfect for entertaining or as an alternative to the usual Sunday roast.

Preheat the oven to 200°C/180°C fan/gas mark 6.

Heat 1 tablespoon of oil in a large deep frying pan. Add the leek with a pinch of salt and fry over a medium heat for around 5 minutes.

In a small bowl, mix the cornflour with a little water to form a loose paste, and set aside.

Add the curry paste and curry powder to the leek and stir to combine. Turn the heat up and add the chicken, drizzling in a little more oil if necessary. Stir-fry for 2–3 minutes, then add the mushrooms and cook for a further 2–3 minutes.

Add the coconut milk, fish sauce and the cornflour mix and simmer for around 5 minutes, or until the chicken is cooked, stirring occasionally,

Taste the sauce and add any extra seasoning, sugar or curry paste if necessary. If adding extra curry paste, simmer for a further couple of minutes. Scatter over the frozen peas and turn off the heat.

Ladle the mixture into a large oven dish (approx. 20 x 30cm) and leave to cool a little. Cover with the puff pastry and use a fork to crimp the edges. Slash two holes in the pastry to allow air to escape, then brush with the beaten egg.

Cook in the oven for 25–30 minutes, or until golden.

Delicious served with mash or my Cumin & Chilli Roast Potatoes (page 174), and a dollop of sour cream or yoghurt, if you like.

> **TIP**
> If making this for young kids, either reduce the curry paste slightly or serve with yoghurt or sour cream to offset the heat.

> **TIP**
> I use May Ploy curry paste, which is spicer and more pungent than many others. If using a different brand, you may need to add more paste and seasoning.

Black Pepper Chicken

Serves:	Prep:	Cook:
2	10 mins	10 mins

A cast of simple storecupboard ingredients comes together to create this lip-smacking stir-fry. Black peppercorns, used as an ingredient – not merely a seasoning – add aromatic pepperiness and heat in addition to the chilli flakes. The holy trinity of garlic, ginger and spring onions forms the base, which together with soy, vinegar and honey creates a satisfyingly savoury-sweet sauce for the succulent chicken. All of this and ready in just 20 minutes!

For the chicken

350g skinless, boneless chicken thighs, cut into 2–3cm cubes

1 tbsp rice vinegar

1 tbsp light soy sauce

1 tsp toasted sesame oil

1 tsp red chilli flakes

2 tbsp cornflour

For the stir-fry

neutral oil, to fry

3 cloves of garlic, finely chopped

1 tbsp grated fresh ginger (approx. 6cm)

2 spring onions, cut into 3cm pieces, greens reserved, thinly sliced

1 tsp freshly ground black pepper

1 tbsp honey

½ tbsp light soy sauce

4 tbsp water

To serve

rice

Delicious with

Tamarind & Honey Green Beans (page 178)

Chilli & Garlic Charred Broccoli (page 182)

Pan-roasted Soy & Black Pepper Fennel (page 176)

Place the chicken in a dish and add the rice vinegar, 1 tablespoon of soy, the sesame oil, red chilli flakes and cornflour. Combine and set aside while you prepare the rest of the ingredients.

Heat 1 tablespoon of oil in a large frying pan over a high heat. Once very hot, add the chicken, leaving behind any excess marinade for later. Stir-fry for 2–3 minutes, until browned all over. Remove from the pan.

Add another tablespoon of oil and tip in the garlic, ginger and spring onions. Stir-fry for 1 minute, then add the black pepper and fry for another 30 seconds or so.

Return the chicken to the pan, along with the reserved marinade. Add the honey, soy and 4 tablespoons of water. Stir-fry for a couple of minutes, or until the chicken is cooked through. Taste and add a drop of soy and/or black pepper if necessary.

Serve with rice, and garnished with the reserved spring onion greens.

T
I
P

This is a relatively spicy dish – if you prefer less heat, use ¼ or ½ teaspoon of chilli flakes instead.

Korean Chicken & Kimchi Rice Traybake

Serves:	Prep:	Cook:
4	15 mins	55 mins

For the marinade & sauce

3 tbsp gochujang
2 tbsp honey
1 tbsp light soy sauce
1 tbsp rice vinegar
1 tbsp ketchup

For the traybake

250g basmati rice
550ml chicken stock
1 tbsp light soy sauce
6–8 chicken thighs (approx. 1kg), bone-in, skin-on, excess fat trimmed
150g kimchi
100g frozen peas

To serve

lime wedges
spring onions, sliced

Delicious with

Soy & Sesame Cucumber Pickle (page 189)

All the flavours of two favourites – Korean chicken and kimchi rice – but in an easy traybake. The addictive sweet and spicy gochujang sauce serves both as a marinade and a drizzling sauce, while the tangy kimchi rice, dotted with peas for added freshness, becomes gorgeously crunchy in bits (which we always fight over!).

Although it takes longer than some of my other dishes, most of the work is done in the oven, making it a great fuss-free meal.

Preheat the oven to 200°C/180°C fan/gas mark 6.

Combine all the ingredients for the marinade and sauce in a small bowl.

Put the rice and stock into a large baking tray and stir in 1 tablespoon of the marinade along with 1 tablespoon of soy.

Spoon 3 tablespoons of the marinade over the chicken and coat. Place the chicken on top of the rice and cover tightly with foil. Bake in the oven for 40 minutes. Remove from the oven and discard the foil. Place the chicken on a plate while you stir through the kimchi and peas.

The rice should have absorbed most of the stock but should still be a bit moist. If it looks very dry, add a splash more. Place the chicken back on top and bake, uncovered, for another 15 minutes, or until the chicken is cooked. If you prefer crispier skin, turn the grill to high and cook for a minute or two until done to your liking.

Add 1 teaspoon of water to the remaining marinade to make a drizzling sauce.

Serve the chicken and rice with wedges of lime, sliced spring onions and with the sauce on the side.

TIP

If your chicken thighs are on the larger side they may take longer than the time given.

Soy & Star Anise Braised Chicken

Serves:
3–4
as part
of a larger
meal

Prep:
5 mins

Cook:
20 mins

neutral oil

6 cloves of garlic, finely chopped

2 tbsp finely chopped fresh coriander stalks

2 tsp freshly ground black pepper

600g skinless, boneless chicken thighs

1 tbsp sugar

2 tbsp light soy sauce

2 tbsp oyster sauce

2 star anise

2 sticks of cinnamon

150ml water

To serve
fresh coriander leaves
rice

Delicious with
Chilli & Garlic Charred Broccoli (page 182)

This recipe is inspired by the aromatic, savoury-sweet Thai dish moo hong, which consists of slow-cooked pork, often belly, simmered in a mixture of garlic, soy, palm sugar and spices. Using skinless, boneless chicken thighs instead of pork means it's ready in a fraction of the time, but the fragrant star anise and cinnamon still come through. Simple but absolutely delicious.

Heat 1 tablespoon of oil in a large saucepan over a medium heat. Add the garlic, coriander stalks and black pepper, and stir-fry for around a minute.

Add a drizzle more oil along with the chicken and turn up the heat slightly. Coat the chicken in the garlic mixture and cook for a few minutes on each side until browned.

Add the remaining ingredients and cover the pan. Bring to a simmer and cook for 7–10 minutes, until the chicken is nearly done. Remove the lid and simmer for a further 5 minutes or so, until the chicken is completely cooked and the sauce is slightly reduced.

Scatter over the coriander leaves and serve with rice.

TIP
If your bunch of coriander doesn't come with long stalks, use a mixture of stalks and leaves. If, on the other hand, you're able to get hold of coriander root, use this instead.

Lemongrass Chicken & Sweet Potato Traybake with Sambal

Serves: 4 **Prep:** 20 mins **Cook:** 40 mins

In this mouth-watering traybake, chicken thighs are marinated in lemongrass and turmeric in a nod to the Indonesian street food dish, smashed chicken or ayam penyet. Instead of the traditional frying, here the thighs are roasted with cubes of sweet potato, then topped with a quick but vibrant spicy tomato sambal, giving layers of flavour and texture.

For the traybake

2 lemongrass stalks
4 cloves of garlic, finely chopped
1 tsp ground turmeric
1 tsp chilli flakes
4 tbsp light soy sauce
6–8 chicken thighs (approx. 1kg), bone-in, skin-on, excess fat trimmed
750g sweet potatoes, skin on, cut into 2–3 cm chunks
2 onions, cut into wedges
2 tbsp neutral oil
sea salt flakes

For the sambal

2–3 mild red chillies (approx. 50–60g), roughly chopped – deseed for a milder heat
2 medium tomatoes, roughly chopped
4 cloves of garlic, roughly chopped
1 onion, roughly chopped
1 tbsp neutral oil
1 tsp sugar
½ tsp salt
a squeeze of fresh lime juice

To serve

fresh coriander leaves
wedges of lime

Preheat the oven to 200°C/180°C fan/gas mark 6.

Remove any tough outer leaves from the lemongrass, then bash the inner ones with a rolling pin. Finely slice them and place it in a dish large enough to fit the chicken.

Add the garlic, turmeric, chilli flakes and soy, and combine. Add the chicken thighs and coat well. Leave to marinate while you prepare the remaining ingredients.

Place the sweet potatoes and onions in a large roasting tin and drizzle over 2 tablespoons of oil. Toss to coat and sprinkle over a good pinch of salt. Place the chicken in the roasting tin, discarding any leftover marinade. Scrape off any lemongrass from the skin, and sprinkle each thigh with salt. Bake for 35–45 minutes, or until the potatoes are tender, the chicken is cooked and its skin is crispy.

Meanwhile, make the sambal. Place the chillies, tomatoes, garlic and onion in a small food processor and blitz until you have a rough paste.

Heat 1 tablespoon of oil in a frying pan over a medium heat, then add the paste along with the sugar and salt. Stir-fry for 5–10 minutes, or until the sambal has thickened and reduced slightly. Taste and add any extra salt or sugar as needed, along with a squeeze of lime juice. Remove from the heat and set aside.

Serve the traybake with the sambal, coriander leaves and wedges of lime.

Chilli Sesame Chicken Stir-fry

Serves:
2

Prep:
15 mins

Cook:
15 mins

A storecupboard raid led me to this nutty, spicy, entirely delicious stir-fry. Using tahini, hoisin and sriracha as its base, it actually reminds me a little of a Thai panang curry. The tahini provides richness and creaminess in place of coconut milk, the hoisin lends sweet and savoury notes, while the sriracha gives a boost of garlicky heat. A simple but triumphant dish!

For the sauce

1½ tbsp hoisin sauce

1 tbsp tahini

1½ tbsp sriracha

½ tbsp honey

½ tsp light soy sauce

½ tsp rice vinegar

2 cloves of garlic, finely chopped

2 tsp grated fresh ginger (approx. 4cm)

½–1 red chilli, finely chopped (deseed for a milder heat)

50ml water

For the stir-fry

40g cashew nuts

1 tbsp neutral oil

250g skinless, boneless chicken thighs, thinly sliced

½ a red pepper, sliced

1 small onion, sliced

60g mangetout

sea salt flakes

To serve

fresh coriander leaves

rice

Delicious with

Quick Radish Pickle with Garlic, Ginger & Chilli (page 191)

Combine the ingredients for the sauce and set near the stove.

Heat a large frying pan or wok over a medium heat and add the cashews. Cook for 2–3 minutes, until lightly toasted and golden. Remove and set aside.

Add 1 tablespoon of oil to the pan and increase the heat to high. When the oil is hot, add the chicken and stir-fry for 2–3 minutes, until the chicken is browned. Add the red pepper, onion and mangetout and stir-fry for 1 minute.

Reduce the heat to medium-high and pour in the sauce. Combine well and stir-fry for another 2 minutes, or until the chicken is cooked through. Taste and add a pinch of salt or a dash of soy if necessary. Stir through the cashew nuts and serve immediately, with coriander leaves and rice.

Thai Green Chicken & Mango Flatbread

Serves: 2

Prep: 20 mins

Cook: 20 mins

For the chicken
2 tbsp natural yoghurt
1 tbsp Thai green curry paste
4 skinless, boneless chicken thighs (approx. 250–300g)
1 tbsp neutral oil

For the onions
½ a red onion, thinly sliced
2 tbsp rice vinegar
sea salt flakes

For the flatbreads (or use shop-bought)
150g self-raising flour
¼ tsp salt
90–100ml water

For the coriander chutney
50g fresh coriander
2 tbsp lime juice (1–1½ limes)
1 small clove of garlic, roughly chopped
1 green or red chilli, roughly chopped (deseed for a milder heat)
2 tsp fish sauce
1 tsp sugar
1 tbsp neutral oil
a pinch of sea salt flakes, to taste

To serve
natural yoghurt
½ a mango, peeled and cut into small cubes
a squeeze of lime juice
fresh coriander

One of my favourite after-pub eats when I first moved to London was a chicken tikka naan wrap – naan bread stuffed with chicken, mint yoghurt and mango chutney – so good! This is my ode to that kebab favourite, but with a Thai twist.

In a dish, mix together the yoghurt and curry paste, then add the chicken. Coat well and set aside to marinate.

Preheat the oven to 110°C/90°C fan/lowest gas mark setting.

Put the red onion, vinegar and a pinch of salt into a small bowl and combine. Set aside.

Put the flour and salt into a mixing bowl and mix in most of the water until a dough forms. You may not need to use it all. If it is too wet, add a sprinkle more flour. Knead for a minute or two, until you have a soft, pliable dough. Cover and set aside.

Place all the ingredients for the coriander chutney in a mini food processor or the jug of a hand blender and blitz. Taste and add any extra sugar or salt as needed.

Divide the dough into two balls. On a floured surface, roll out the balls into discs approx. 3mm thick. Heat a large frying pan on high and when hot, place a flatbread in the pan. Cook for 1–2 minutes on each side until they start to puff up and become golden. Put the flatbreads on an ovenproof plate or dish and cover with another plate or some foil. Place in the oven to keep warm while you cook the chicken.

Add 1 tablespoon of oil to the pan and reduce the heat to medium-high. Add the chicken and cook for 5 minutes on each side. Leave to rest for a minute or two before slicing.

To serve, spread a dollop of yoghurt on each wrap and top with the sliced chicken, coriander chutney, mango, pickled red onion, a squeeze of lime and fresh coriander leaves.

Chicken & Mushroom Oyakodon

Serves:
2

Prep:
5 mins

Cook:
15 mins

200ml chicken stock

2 tbsp mirin (or use 2 tbsp rice vinegar + 1 tsp sugar)

2 tbsp soy sauce

1 tsp sugar

1 small onion, finely sliced

150g skinless, boneless chicken thighs, thinly sliced

100g chestnut mushrooms, thinly sliced

2 eggs, beaten

It is a wonder how some ingredients come together so effortlessly to create a dish that is greater than the sum of its parts. Oyakodon, a Japanese dish of chicken and egg does just that. Deceptively simple and quick, this is the one-pot meal you want when you're craving something gentle, yet satisfying.

The chicken, egg and onion, along with the untraditional addition of mushrooms, simmer in a mirin and soy-based stock, which brings out the savoury-sweet notes of the ingredients. It is meant to be 'liquidy' and is served on a bed of rice.

Put the stock, mirin, soy and sugar into a medium-sized frying pan over a high heat and bring to the boil. Lower the heat to medium, then add the sliced onions in a layer, followed by the chicken and mushrooms. Simmer for 5–10 minutes, until the chicken and mushrooms are cooked.

Taste the broth and add any extra soy or sugar. It should be well balanced.

Pour the eggs evenly over the chicken and mushrooms, and cook until just set but still slightly runny in the centre. Don't stir the eggs.

Serve immediately, over rice.

T
I
P

Don't overcook the eggs. They should be cooked until just set, with a creamy, soft texture.

beef, pork & lamb

Sticky Hoisin Beef

Serves:
4

Prep:
15 mins

Cook:
15–20 mins

You can never have too many fakeaway dishes up your sleeve to make those nights in a bit more special. This dish has all the flavours you would expect from your favourite Chinese – think sweet and sticky hoisin, aromatic Chinese 5-spice, garlic and ginger, as well as a little kick from the sriracha. A family favourite.

For the sauce

6 tbsp hoisin sauce

1 tbsp sriracha

¼ tsp Chinese 5-spice

¼ tsp chilli flakes (optional)

2 tsp rice wine or white wine vinegar

125ml water

For the stir-fry

2 x sirloin steak, (approx. 450g), thinly sliced

3 tbsp cornflour

¼ tsp fine salt

neutral oil, to fry

1 onion, sliced

4 cloves of garlic, finely chopped

2 tsp grated fresh ginger (approx. 4cm)

175g broccoli, cut into small florets

To serve

rice

1 spring onion, finely sliced

1 red chilli, finely sliced (optional)

Delicious with

Soy & Sesame Cucumber Pickle (page 189)

Mix together the ingredients for the sauce and set aside.

Place the steak in a dish or mixing bowl and add the cornflour and salt. Coat well, making sure every piece is separated out.

Heat 2 tablespoons of oil in a large non-stick frying pan over a high heat. Once very hot, add the steak, separating the pieces as you go. Fry for 3–5 minutes, or until golden and crisp all over, leaving it untouched for the first 1–2 minutes to help it colour. Remove from the pan. You may need to do this in batches.

Scrape out any burnt bits and reduce the heat to medium-high. Add 1 tablespoon of oil to the pan, then tip in the onion, garlic and ginger. Cook for 1 minute or so, then add the broccoli. Stir-fry for 2–3 minutes, until the broccoli is almost cooked.

Pour in the sauce and bubble briefly, then put back the beef along with any juices. Coat well in the sauce. Taste and add any extra seasoning as necessary.

Serve immediately with rice, and scattered with spring onion and chilli, if using.

 If making it for younger kids, omit the chilli flakes and reduce the sriracha to 1–2 teaspoons.

Sweet & Sour Tamarind Pork & Pineapple

Serves:	Prep:	Cook:
2	10 mins	10 mins

2 thin pork loin steaks, (approx. 250g), thinly sliced

1 tbsp cornflour

1 tbsp light soy sauce

neutral oil, to fry

2 spring onions, cut into 4cm pieces

1 red pepper, thinly sliced

2 cloves of garlic, finely chopped

2cm slice of fresh pineapple (approx. 200g unpeeled weight), cut into small bite-size pieces

sea salt flakes

For the sauce

1 tsp cornflour

100ml water

3 tbsp tamarind paste (see pages 20–21)

3–3½ tbsp soft brown sugar (depending on how sweet you like it)

2 tsp fish sauce

To serve

fresh coriander leaves (optional)

rice

A riff on the beloved classic sweet and sour pork, this recipe uses tamarind, which lends a deliciously tangy and fruity note to the dish.

Ready in less time than it takes to scroll through a takeaway menu, this is a fantastic fakeaway meal to add to your repertoire!

Place the pork in a small dish and add the cornflour and soy. Combine well, then leave to marinate while you prepare the rest of the ingredients.

For the sauce, mix together the cornflour with a little of the water to form a paste, then stir in the remaining water along with the rest of the sauce ingredients. Stir until the sugar dissolves. Place near the stove.

Heat 1 tablespoon of oil over a high heat and once very hot, add the pork, being sure to separate all the pieces. Fry for 2 minutes, or until browned, leaving it untouched for the first minute or so. Remove from the pan and set aside.

Add another tablespoon of oil to the pan, then tip in the spring onions and red pepper. Stir-fry for 1 minute, then add the garlic. Stir-fry for a further 30 seconds or so, then add the pineapple and the sauce.

Reduce the heat and simmer for a minute or so. Return the pork and cook for another minute, or until the pork is cooked through. Taste and add a pinch of salt, or a little extra sugar if necessary. Scatter over the coriander leaves, if using, and serve immediately, with rice.

TIP Marinate the pork first, before preparing the rest of the ingredients.

VEGAN Swap the fish sauce for soy, and the pork for crispy fried tofu (see page 98).

Spicy Sausage & Kale Gnocchi

Serves:
4

Prep:
10 mins

Cook:
15 mins

For the sauce
3 tbsp gochujang
1 tbsp honey
3 cloves of garlic, crushed
1 tbsp rice vinegar
1 tbsp light soy sauce
1 tsp chilli flakes (optional)
200ml water

For the gnocchi
1 tbsp neutral oil
6 sausages, cut into small
    pieces
500g shop-bought gnocchi
100g kale or spring greens,
    finely shredded

Shop-bought gnocchi is a brilliant ingredient to have on hand. It's ready in just a few minutes, so I often reach for it when I need a last-minute speedy dinner. This recipe uses the mighty gochujang to create a warm and spicy sauce, which couldn't be more perfect with all that squidgy gnocchi. Combined with sausages and kale, we have a rich and hearty one-pot dish that makes you want to dive in!

Mix together all the ingredients for the sauce, apart from the water, until combined. Stir in the water and set aside.

Heat 1 tablespoon of oil in a large deep frying pan over a medium heat. Add the sausages and fry for 6–7 minutes, until browned and mostly cooked, turning occasionally. Add the gnocchi and fry for a couple of minutes.

Tip in the kale or spring greens and fry for a further 2 minutes, until beginning to wilt.

Pour in the sauce and bubble for a couple of minutes until the greens are wilted and the sausages are cooked. Serve immediately.

VEGAN
Swap the sausages for mushrooms and the honey for agave syrup.

Chinese 5-Spice Lamb & Plums

Serves:
4

Prep:
10 mins

Cook:
20 mins

4 lamb leg steaks (approx.
   450–500g)
sea salt flakes
black pepper
neutral oil, to fry
2 cloves of garlic, crushed
2 tsp grated fresh ginger
   (approx. 4cm)
250g plums, stones removed,
   cut into wedges
2 tbsp honey
¼ tsp Chinese 5-spice
zest of 1 orange
50ml orange juice
   (approx. half an orange)
1 tsp rice vinegar
½ tsp light soy sauce
3 tbsp water

To serve
rice
2 spring onions, finely sliced

Chinese 5-spice plums, often paired with duck, marry brilliantly with lamb steaks instead in this fruity and aromatic one-pot dish.

The sweet and tart plums mingle with orange, garlic, ginger and honey to create a sweet and sour sauce gutsy enough to balance out the rich lamb. Simple enough to upgrade your midweek dinner, but equally impressive to serve to guests.

Season the lamb well with sea salt flakes and black pepper.

Heat 1 tablespoon of oil in a large deep frying pan over a medium-high heat. When hot, add the lamb steaks and cook for 2–3 minutes or so on each side, until browned and just cooked. Try not to touch for the first couple of minutes, to allow a crust to form. Remove.

Reduce the heat slightly and add 1 tablespoon of oil to the pan. Fry the garlic and ginger for 1 minute or so, then add the plums with the rest of the ingredients.

Simmer for around 3–5 minutes, stirring occasionally, until the plums are soft (but still hold their shape) and the sauce has reduced slightly. Add a splash more water if it becomes too thick. Taste the sauce and add any extra soy or seasoning as needed. If your plums are on the tart side you may need to add a little more honey or a pinch of sugar.

Put the lamb steaks back into the pan, coat in the sauce and cook for a minute to warm through if needed.

Serve with rice and scatter over the spring onions.

 T I P To prepare in advance, make the sauce as per the recipe, but only simmer for a couple of minutes. Refrigerate until needed. Before serving, cook the meat as instructed. Bring the prepared sauce to a simmer and follow the remaining instructions.

 T I P You may need to adjust the timings for cooking the lamb, depending on the thickness of your steaks.

Vietnamese-style Caramel Pork Stir-fry

Serves:	Prep:	Cook:
4	15 mins	10–15 mins

For the stir-fry

1 x 450g pork fillet, thinly
   sliced
1 tbsp cornflour
1 tbsp fish sauce
1 tbsp soy sauce
neutral oil, to fry
1 onion, sliced
4 cloves of garlic, finely
   chopped
100g broccoli, cut into
   small bite-size florets
1 red pepper, sliced

For the sauce

3 tbsp soft brown sugar
3 tbsp water
2 tbsp fish sauce
1 tbsp rice vinegar

To serve

rice

This easy stir-fry harnesses the sweet and savoury flavours of Vietnamese caramel pork, typically a slow-cooked dish using pork belly or pork shoulder. The pork fillet cooks in a fraction of the time and is perfectly tender, thanks to the simple marinade of cornflour, soy and fish sauce. Brown sugar provides the caramel element, while the addition of broccoli and red pepper adds a welcome freshness. An inauthentic take on a traditional dish, but totally delicious!

Put the pork into a dish and add the cornflour, fish sauce and soy. Toss to coat. Leave to marinate while you prepare the vegetables.

Combine the ingredients for the sauce in a small bowl and set near the stove.

Heat 1 tablespoon of oil in a large non-stick frying pan over a high heat. Once the oil is hot, add the pork and fry for a couple of minutes, until browned but not completely cooked through. Remove along with any bits stuck to the pan – reserve them with the pork, unless they are burnt. You may need to do this in batches.

Heat another tablespoon of oil and add the onions and garlic. Stir-fry for a minute, then add the broccoli and red pepper. Stir-fry for a couple of minutes, until tender-crisp. Add the sauce and reduce the heat slightly. Bubble for a few moments, then put back the pork. Coat well in the sauce and cook for a couple of minutes, or until the pork is cooked through. Serve immediately, with rice.

Satay BLT

Serves:
2

Prep:
10 mins

Cook:
10 mins

For the sandwich

4 slices of sourdough or
preferred bread

6–8 rashers of smoked
streaky bacon (depending
on appetite)

1–2 tomatoes (depending
on the size)

lettuce leaves

For the sauce

5 tbsp crunchy, unsweetened
peanut butter

1½ tbsp sweet chilli sauce

1½ tbsp sriracha

2 tsp rice wine vinegar

½ tsp soy sauce

I must have satay sauce on the brain – I could eat it with almost anything. One Saturday I had a fancy for a BLT and thought the salty bacon would work perfectly smothered in a creamy, sweet and slightly spicy peanut sauce – I was right. Satay lovers will love this!

Preheat your grill to high. Place the bacon on a baking sheet lined with foil. If you have a grill rack, sit your bacon on top. Cook for 5–10 minutes, until crispy.

Meanwhile, combine the ingredients for the sauce in a small bowl. Add a teaspoon of water at a time to achieve a 'dolloping' consistency.

To assemble, toast your sourdough, then spread the sauce on each slice. Layer with bacon, tomatoes and lettuce. Dive in.

T I P
I love the amount of sauce given in the recipe, but if you have any left over you can add it to a noodle stir-fry, add stock to make a creamy ramen-style noodle broth, or use it as a dip for prawns, summer rolls or even tortilla chips!

V E G A N
Swap the bacon for crispy fried tofu (see page 98, but cut the tofu into slices).

veg, eggs & tofu mains

Manchurian Cauliflower Traybake

Serves:
2–3

Prep:
15 mins

Cook:
20–25 mins

1 medium cauliflower
(approx. 600g prepared
weight), cut into bite-size
florets

1 red onion, cut into thin
wedges

2 red peppers, cut into thick
strips

2 tbsp neutral oil

sea salt flakes

For the sauce

3 tbsp light soy sauce

3 tbsp ketchup

2 tbsp rice vinegar

2 tbsp sriracha

1½ tbsp honey

75ml water

1 tbsp neutral oil

4 cloves of garlic, finely
chopped

1 tbsp grated fresh ginger
(approx. 6cm)

1 red chilli, finely chopped
(deseed for a milder heat)

3 spring onions, sliced

To serve

spring onions, sliced, or
coriander leaves

rice

*This easy traybake combines a tangy, spicy Manchurian sauce
with roasted cauliflower and peppers for a flavour-packed meal.
'Manchurian' is a popular Indo-Chinese dish often featuring
vegetables, chicken or meatballs, and has a savoury sweetness.
Roasting the cauliflower at a high temperature chars it slightly
and brings out its nutty, sweet flavour, which works so well with
the garlicky ginger-based sauce.*

Preheat the oven to 240°C/220°C fan/gas mark 9.

Place the cauliflower, onion and red peppers in a large roasting
tray. Drizzle over 2 tablespoons of oil and add a good pinch of salt.
Roast for 20–25 minutes, until the cauliflower is starting to char and
the pepper is soft, turning halfway.

Meanwhile, make the sauce. Mix the soy, ketchup, vinegar, sriracha,
honey and water in a small bowl and set near the stove.

Heat 1 tablespoon of oil in a frying pan over a medium heat and fry
the garlic, ginger, chilli and spring onions for 1–2 minutes, until
softened. Add the sauce and simmer for 2 minutes, or until
thickened and syrupy.

Once the vegetables are cooked, remove from the oven and
pour over the sauce. Toss to coat. Scatter over the spring onions
or coriander, and serve with rice.

T
I
P
If you like it spicy, feel
free to add another chilli
to the sauce.

Thai Green Curry Fried Rice

Serves:
2

Prep:
5 mins

Cook:
10 mins

neutral oil, to fry
2 eggs, beaten
1 medium leek, finely sliced
1 tbsp Thai green (or red) curry paste (see tip)
50ml milk, coconut milk if you have it, or any other milk
100g peas (I use frozen)
250g cooked rice (approx. 110g uncooked weight of jasmine rice or 90g of basmati)
1 tsp fish sauce or light soy sauce

To serve (optional)
lime wedges
fresh coriander leaves

Fried rice is on my menu at least once a week – I just love its versatility and speed. A popular dish in Thailand, this recipe is a delicious way to use up leftover curry paste (despite its name it also works brilliantly with red), as well as any veg.

It is a slightly wetter stir-fry, so make sure your rice isn't too wet to begin with. If so, you may need to spread it out and chill it in the fridge to help dry it out.

Heat 1 tablespoon of oil in a large frying pan or wok over a high heat. When hot, pour in the beaten eggs. Lightly scramble, then push to the side of the pan (if possible, moving that side of the pan slightly off the heat).

Add another 1 tablespoon of oil, then add the leek. Stir-fry for 2–3 minutes, until softened. Again move to the side of the pan, and turn the heat down to medium.

Drizzle in a little more oil, then add the curry paste. Stir-fry for 30 seconds or so, until it starts to become fragrant. Stir in the milk and bubble for a few moments. Mix in the leek and eggs, and tip in the peas. Add the rice, along with the fish sauce or soy. Increase the heat slightly, and combine well.

Once the rice is hot, taste and add any extra soy or fish sauce, if necessary. Serve immediately, with lime wedges or coriander leaves.

 TIP I use May Ploy curry paste, which is spicer and more pungent than many others. If using a different brand, you may need to add more paste and seasoning.

 SWITCH Feel free to add whatever veg you have to hand, or try adding prawns or left-over chicken.

Spicy Tomato & Egg Soup

| Serves:
2 | Prep:
5 mins | Cook:
10 mins |

1 tbsp neutral oil

2 spring onions, sliced
(greens reserved for
garnish)

2 cloves of garlic, finely
chopped

1 tsp grated fresh ginger
(approx. 2cm)

1 red chilli, halved and sliced
(deseed for a milder heat)

3 medium ripe tomatoes,
finely chopped

1 tsp sugar

1 tbsp fish sauce

500ml vegetable stock

2 eggs

To serve

spring onion greens, sliced

fresh coriander leaves

chilli oil (optional)

Tomato soup is always a winner in my household – it never fails to hit the spot when comfort and warmth are needed. This Asian-inspired version uses spring onions, garlic, ginger and chillis, alongside sautéed tomatoes for a deliciously aromatic bowl of goodness. The egg adds creaminess and works so well with the tomatoes. My kids love this but without the chillis!

Heat the oil in a large, deep, lidded frying pan or wok over a medium-high heat. Add the spring onions, garlic, ginger and chilli and stir-fry for a minute or so, until aromatic.

Add the tomatoes and cook for another couple of minutes, stirring occasionally, until slightly softened. Add the sugar, fish sauce and stock and bring to the boil. Bubble for a couple of minutes. Taste and add any extra fish sauce or sugar.

Reduce the heat to medium, then crack in the eggs and put the lid on the pan. Simmer for 3 minutes, or until the eggs are done to your liking.

Divide the soup between two bowls, and top with the eggs (being careful not to break them). Garnish with the spring onion greens and coriander leaves, and chilli oil, if you fancy.

V E G G I E
Swap the fish sauce for light soy sauce.

Savoury Porridge with Garlic Mushrooms & Spring Onion Oil

Serves: 2   **Prep:** 10 mins   **Cook:** 15 mins

100g porridge oats

750ml chicken or vegetable stock

2 tsp white miso paste (or substitute light soy sauce)

light soy sauce, to taste

For the mushrooms

neutral oil, to fry

150g chestnut mushrooms, thinly sliced

sea salt flakes

2 cloves of garlic, finely chopped

For the spring onion oil

1 spring onion, finely chopped

2 cloves of garlic, finely chopped

1 tbsp salted peanuts, chopped

1 tsp chilli flakes

2 tbsp neutral oil

sea salt flakes

If you've never tasted savoury porridge, it may seem like a strange idea. However, if you are a fan of the usual breakfast variety, I urge you to give this a go. Along similar lines to Asian rice soups like congee and khao tom (see page 162), this dish is both comforting and calming. The porridge itself has a subtle flavour, making it a perfect base for any toppings. The mushrooms and spring onions here are merely a serving suggestion – the possibilities are endless.

Place the oats and stock in a saucepan over a high heat and bring to the boil. Reduce the heat and simmer for around 4–5 minutes, stirring occasionally, until the oats are cooked. Feel free to add a little more stock or water if you prefer it looser.

Meanwhile, cook the mushrooms. Heat 1 tablespoon of oil in a frying pan over a high heat. Fry the mushrooms, along with a pinch of salt, for a few minutes until they are golden, stirring occasionally. Add a drizzle more oil if necessary, then add the garlic. Fry for a minute or two until the garlic is golden, then take off the heat.

Place all the ingredients for the spring onion oil, apart from the oil and salt, in a small bowl. Heat the oil in a small saucepan on medium-high for 1 minute or so, until bubbles appear (if you put a wooden chopstick or a piece of garlic into the oil, it should sizzle). When hot, pour the oil into the bowl. Combine and add a pinch of salt to taste.

Once the porridge is cooked, stir through your miso paste, making sure it dissolves. Taste and adjust the seasoning by adding a little more miso or a few drops of soy (remembering that the spring onion oil will also be salty).

To serve, divide the porridge between two bowls. Top with the mushrooms and drizzle over the spring onion oil.

TIP If your spring onions and garlic are large, increase the amount of oil to 3–4 tablespoons. Any leftovers can be kept in the fridge and used to jazz up noodles and rice dishes.

TIP I use porridge oats (often called 'rolled oats') as opposed to jumbo oats, as these cook more quickly. You may need to adjust your timings if using the latter.

Sweet & Spicy Crispy Tofu

Serves:
2

Prep:
5 mins

Cook:
15 mins

If you've never had tofu or think you don't like it, read on! Tofu when cooked badly isn't the most inspiring thing in the world, I admit. But when crispy-fried, then coated in an umami-rich, garlicky, sweet and spicy sauce, as it is here, it's a whole other story. If you love those flavours, I promise this dish will convert you!

For the sauce
1 tsp cornflour
100ml water
1–2 tbsp chilli bean paste (see tip)
1–1½ tbsp honey

For the stir-fry
200g extra firm tofu, patted dry
2 tbsp cornflour
neutral oil, to fry
½ a red pepper, thinly sliced
100g broccoli, cut into small bite-size florets
2 spring onions, cut into 4cm pieces

To serve
1 spring onion, finely sliced (optional)
rice

Make the sauce. In a small bowl mix together the cornflour with 1 tablespoon of the water until you have a paste. Mix in the chilli bean paste, 1 tablespoon of honey and the rest of the 100ml of water. Set near the stove.

Tear the tofu into bite-size pieces and place in a bowl. Don't worry if some of it breaks up a bit – this will add great texture. Sprinkle over the cornflour and toss to coat.

Heat 1 tablespoon of oil in a large non-stick frying pan or wok over a medium-high heat, and when very hot, add the tofu. Cook for around 5 minutes, until golden and crispy, turning occasionally, but leaving it untouched for the first 1–2 minutes. Remove from the pan.

Add another 1 tablespoon of oil, then tip in the pepper, broccoli and spring onions. Stir-fry for 2 minutes, or until the broccoli is almost cooked, then add the sauce. Reduce the heat slightly and bubble for a few moments, until the sauce has thickened and the broccoli is just cooked. If it seems a little dry, add a splash of water. Taste and add any extra honey or chilli bean paste if necessary.

Put the tofu back into the pan and coat in the sauce. Serve immediately, with rice and sprinkled with spring onions, if using.

TIP If you can't get hold of chilli bean paste, use 1 tablespoon each of white miso paste and sriracha with ¼ teaspoon of chilli flakes.

TIP The saltiness of chilli bean paste brands varies. I use Lee Kum Kee, which is less salty than others. If using another brand, start off with 1 tablespoon and add more if necessary (see page 14).

Thai Rice Soup with Fried Eggs & Crispy Capers

Serves: 2

Prep: 10 mins

Cook: 15–20 mins

For the rice

1 stalk of lemongrass

2 tbsp neutral oil

4 cloves of garlic, finely chopped

900ml vegetable or chicken stock

4–6 thick slices of fresh ginger, skin on

100g uncooked jasmine or basmati rice

For the toppings

1–2 mild red chillies, finely sliced (according to taste)

3–4 tbsp rice vinegar or white wine vinegar

neutral oil, to fry

2 tbsp capers, drained and dried well

2 eggs

a few cornichons, sliced

To serve

a small handful of fresh coriander leaves, roughly chopped

fish sauce and/or light soy sauce, optional (taste first – remember the capers are salty!)

Khao tom – a comforting rice soup made in most households in Thailand – was one of my mother's favourite childhood breakfasts, but is also eaten throughout the day. Once you have the base soup, you can add any toppings or sides you like, such as minced pork, prawns or Thai omelette. In this recipe a simple fried egg turns into something magical with the addition of crispy, salty capers and red chillies in vinegar. Sweet pickled cornichons, crisp fried garlic and fresh coriander round things off deliciously.

Prepare the lemongrass. Remove any tough outer leaves, then bash the inner ones with a rolling pin. Cut in half.

Heat 2 tablespoons of oil in a large pan over a medium-low heat. Fry the garlic for 1–2 minutes, until it just starts to become golden (but no more), stirring frequently. Be careful not to let it burn as it will continue cooking off the heat. Take the pan off the heat for a moment and remove half the garlic, including half the oil, and reserve for the garnish.

Add the stock, lemongrass, ginger and rice, and put the pan back on the stove. Increase the heat and bring to the boil, then reduce the heat and simmer for 10–15 minutes, or until the rice is cooked, stirring occasionally.

Meanwhile, make the toppings. Combine the chillies with the vinegar in a small dish and set aside. Heat 2 tablespoons of oil in a small frying pan over a fairly high heat and when hot, add the capers. Cook for 3–4 minutes, until they become crispy, tossing occasionally. Remove with a slotted spoon and drain on kitchen paper.

Five minutes before the rice is ready, fry the eggs according to your preference.

To serve, divide the soup between two bowls. Top each with a fried egg, capers, cornichons, chopped coriander and the reserved fried garlic. Serve with the chillies in vinegar on the side and fish sauce or soy to add if needed.

TIP I've used uncooked rice, but it can also be made with cooked rice. If using the latter, don't add the rice until after the lemongrass and ginger have simmered for 10 minutes. Cook the rice until hot through. You will need around 200–250g cooked rice for this.

VEGAN Use vegetable stock, and swap the egg for fried leafy greens.

Korean Sweet Potato, Chickpea & Spring Green Stew

Serves:
4

Prep:
10 mins

Cook:
25 mins

2 tbsp neutral oil

1 onion, finely chopped

4 cloves of garlic, finely chopped

1 tbsp grated fresh ginger (approx. 6cm)

750ml veg or chicken stock

2 tbsp gochujang

2 tbsp rice wine vinegar

1 tbsp light soy sauce

1 tbsp toasted sesame oil

2 tsp honey

500g sweet potatoes, peeled and cut into 2–3cm chunks

1 x 400g tin of chickpeas, drained

100g spring greens (or other leafy greens), shredded

salt and pepper

Delicious with
Tangy Pickled Cabbage (page 188)

Inspired by a delicious Korean chicken stew known as dak-dori-tang, this recipe instead uses sweet potatoes and chickpeas to soak up the rich gochujang-based broth. With added garlic, ginger, honey and soy, this dish isn't shy on flavour – bold yet comforting and with the right amount of sweet and spice. Just the ticket when you want something that tastes as good as it makes you feel!

Heat 2 tablespoons of oil in a large saucepan over a medium heat. Add the onion and cook for 3 minutes, stirring occasionally, until starting to soften. Add the garlic and ginger and cook for another couple of minutes.

Pour in the stock, then add the gochujang, vinegar, soy, sesame oil and honey, followed by the sweet potatoes and chickpeas. Increase the heat and bring to the boil, then reduce the heat slightly and simmer for 10–15 minutes, or until the sweet potatoes are cooked, stirring occasionally.

Mix in the greens and cook for another minute or so until wilted. Taste the sauce and add any extra honey, soy or seasoning as needed.

SWITCH
Try squash instead of the sweet potatoes, butter beans instead of the chickpeas, and any leafy greens such as spinach or kale instead of the spring greens. Courgettes would work well too. Just be sure to amend the cooking times as necessary.

Sweet Soy Tofu

Serves:	Prep:	Cook:
2	10 mins	15 mins

For the sauce

1½ tbsp light soy sauce

1 tbsp soft brown sugar

1 tbsp honey

75ml/5 tbsp water

For the stir-fry

200g extra firm tofu, cut
  into 4–5cm batons and
  patted dry

2 tbsp cornflour

40g cashews

neutral oil, to fry

1 small onion, sliced

1 red chilli, thinly sliced
  (deseed for a milder heat)

1 tsp grated fresh ginger
  (approx. 2cm)

100g green beans, halved

2 cloves of garlic, finely
  chopped

sea salt flakes

To serve

rice

Lara Lee's recipe for sweet soy tempeh, a popular Indonesian dish, was the inspiration for this simple but stunning stir-fry. Kecap manis, an Indonesian sweet soy sauce, is usually the key ingredient, but isn't that widely available in the supermarket. Once again the storecupboard comes to the rescue, with perhaps the most familiar ingredient of all – light soy sauce. When bubbled with soft brown sugar, the flavour intensifies and acts as a great substitute for the dark and sticky kecap manis.

Combine the ingredients for the sauce in a small bowl and set near the stove.

Place the tofu in a mixing bowl and add the cornflour. Toss to coat.

Heat a large non-stick frying pan on medium-high and add the cashews. Cook for a few minutes, stirring frequently, until golden and toasted. Remove and set aside.

Add 1 tablespoon of oil to the pan, and when very hot add the tofu. Fry for around 5 minutes, until golden, trying not to move the tofu for the first couple of minutes or so. Remove and set aside.

Reduce the heat to medium and heat another 1 tablespoon of oil. Add the onion, chilli and ginger and stir-fry for a couple of minutes. Add the green beans, then the garlic, and stir-fry for 1–2 minutes, until the beans are tender-crisp but not yet cooked.

Add the sauce and bubble for 2 minutes or so, until reduced and syrupy, and the green beans are just cooked. Stir occasionally. Add the tofu and stir-fry until well combined. Taste the sauce and add a pinch of salt or a drop of soy if necessary. Turn off the heat, mix through the cashews and serve immediately, with rice.

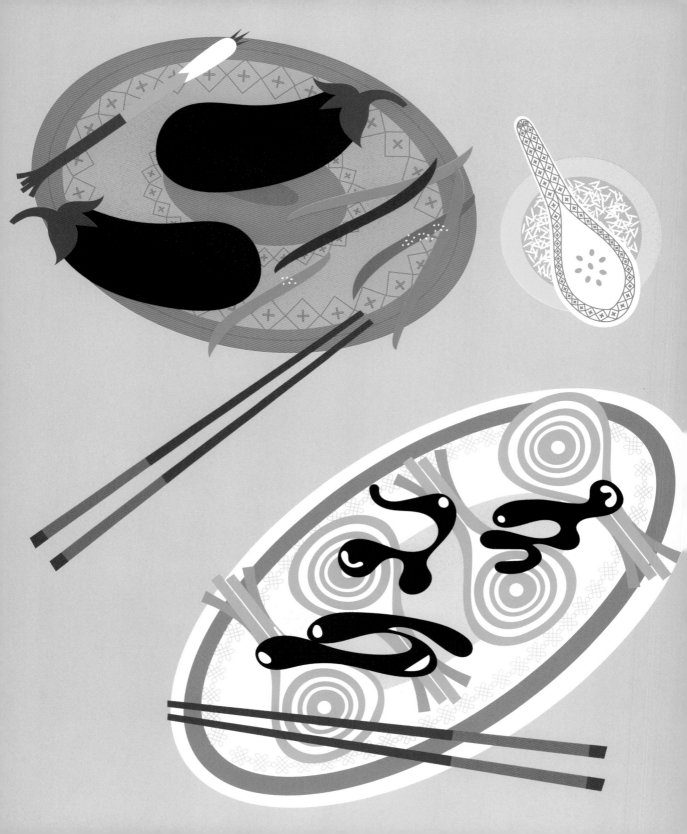

veg

sides

Garlicky Soy Aubergines

Serves: 4

Prep: 10 mins

Cook: 35–40 mins

2 medium aubergines
2–3 tbsp oil (depending on the size of the aubergines)
sea salt flakes

For the dressing
1 tbsp neutral oil
3 spring onions, thinly sliced (reserve half the green parts for garnish)
2 fat garlic cloves, finely chopped
1 tbsp fresh ginger, finely chopped (approx. 6cm)
2 tsp caster sugar
2½ tbsp rice vinegar
1 tbsp light soy sauce
1 tbsp crispy chilli oil, mostly the bits (see page 16)

To serve
spring onion greens, sliced

Delicious with
Chilli Tamarind Prawns with Mangetout (page 114)

This is such a gorgeous way of eating aubergines. Roasted until soft and caramelized, the aubergines are then drizzled with a spicy, sweet and sour dressing made from a few storecupboard staples – soy, rice vinegar, chilli oil and sugar – along with crispy fried garlic, ginger and spring onions. Believe me when I say you'll probably want to eat the whole bowl!

I love it just as much as a side or served on its own with rice.

Preheat the oven to 200°C/180°C fan/gas mark 6.

Prepare the aubergine. Cut each one in half lengthways, then again widthways. Cut each quarter into wedges. Place the aubergine wedges on a baking tray, drizzle over the oil with a good pinch of sea salt, and coat well. Cook for 35–40 minutes, until meltingly tender, turning halfway. Once done, place in a serving dish.

Heat 1 tablespoon of oil in a small frying pan over a medium-high heat. Add the spring onions, garlic and ginger and fry for a couple of minutes, or until the garlic is just golden, stirring frequently. Stir in the sugar and turn off the heat. Add the vinegar, soy and crispy chilli oil, and mix.

Pour the dressing evenly over the aubergine and combine. Scatter with the spring onion greens. Delicious served warm, but can also be enjoyed at room temperature.

Sesame Chilli New Potato Salad

Serves: 4   **Prep:** 5 mins   **Cook:** 20 mins

500g new potatoes, large ones halved or quartered

3 tbsp tahini

3 tbsp crispy chilli oil, mostly the bits (see page 16)

2 tsp light soy sauce

1 tbsp honey

2 tbsp rice vinegar

2 tbsp water

To serve

1 spring onion, finely sliced

The idea for this recipe was sparked by the irresistible sauce used in the classic Sichuan dish, Dan Dan noodles, typically made with sesame paste, chilli oil and soy. I often do a quick version for lunch, just the sauce poured over noodles, cold or warm, with perhaps some spring onions or cucumber for greenery.

In place of noodles here, the potatoes provide an ideal canvas for the creamy and nutty tahini, the spiciness of chilli oil, and the sweet and sour notes of soy, honey and vinegar. The result is completely addictive – I can honestly say this might be the best potato salad I've ever tasted!

Place the potatoes in a large saucepan of boiling salted water. Boil for 15–20 minutes, until completely tender. Drain well and steam dry for 1–2 minutes.

Meanwhile, combine the rest of the ingredients in a large bowl.

Add the potatoes to the dressing and coat. Serve sprinkled with the spring onions. Delicious hot or cold.

Cumin & Chilli Roast Potatoes

Serves: 4–6

Prep: 10 mins

Cook: 30–35 mins

1 kg potatoes, skin on, cut into 2cm pieces

1 tsp chilli powder

1½ tsp ground cumin

½ tsp sea salt flakes

5 tbsp neutral oil

1 bunch of spring onions, finely sliced

6–8 cloves of garlic, finely chopped

2 red chillies, finely chopped (deseeded for a milder heat)

Delicious with

Thai Chicken Curry Pie (page 118)

We love a roast potato in our family. In this recipe they are generously sprinkled with chilli powder and cumin, then, once roasted, tossed with fried spring onions, chillies and crispy garlic. Flavour-packed and very moreish, I sometimes eat them as a main – simply top with a fried egg and a drizzle of chilli oil and you're good to go.

Preheat the oven to 220°C/200°C fan/gas mark 7.

Place the potatoes in a large baking tray and sprinkle over the chilli powder, cumin and salt. Drizzle over 3 tablespoons of the oil and toss to coat. Roast in the oven for 30–35 minutes, or until cooked and golden, turning them halfway through.

Once the potatoes are ready, prepare the spring onion and garlic topping. Heat the remaining 2 tablespoons of oil in a frying pan over a medium-high heat. Add the spring onions, garlic, and chillies. Stir-fry for 2 minutes, or until softened and the garlic becomes golden.

Tip the mixture into the baking tray and combine with the potatoes. Serve immediately.

Pan-roasted Soy & Black Pepper Fennel

Serves:	Prep:	Cook:
4	5 mins	15 mins

For the fennel

2 medium bulbs of fennel (approx. 500–600g total)

1 tbsp neutral oil

For the sauce

3 tbsp light soy sauce

3 tbsp rice vinegar

1 tbsp sugar

1 tsp freshly ground black pepper

¼ tsp chilli flakes

75ml water

Delicious with

Black Pepper Chicken (page 120)

Chinese 5-spice Prawns (page 104)

Fennel's crisp texture and refreshing mild aniseed flavour work so well raw in salads, but I love it just as much when cooked, which showcases its mellower side. In this recipe, the fennel is pan-fried until golden, then simmered in an irresistible mix of black pepper, soy, vinegar, sugar and chillies, becoming soft and slightly caramelized. Gorgeous!

Discard any brown bits from the fennel. Remove the fronds and set aside. Cut off the stalks and slice them lengthways. Slice the bulb into 1cm rounds.

Combine the ingredients for the sauce in a small bowl, stirring to dissolve the sugar. Set near the stove.

Heat 1 tablespoon of oil in a large lidded frying pan over a high heat. Add the fennel and cook for about 5–6 minutes, until golden and starting to char in places, turning occasionally.

Reduce the heat slightly and add the sauce.

Simmer with a lid on for 2–3 minutes, or until softened, then remove the lid and simmer for another minute or so to reduce the sauce slightly. Delicious served hot or warm, topped with the reserved fennel fronds.

Tamarind & Honey Green Beans

Serves:
4

Prep:
5 mins

Cook:
10 mins

Sweet, tangy, savoury, garlicky and nutty all at the same time. A delicious way to switch up your green beans!

For the sauce

2 tbsp honey

2 tbsp tamarind paste
(see pages 20–21)

2 tsp light soy sauce

1 tsp sesame oil

2 tbsp water

For the stir-fry

neutral oil, to fry

400g green beans

4 cloves of garlic, finely
chopped

To serve

2 tbsp sesame seeds, toasted
(optional)

Delicious with

Black Pepper Chicken
(page 120)

Chilli Tamarind Prawns with
Mangetout (page 114)

Combine the ingredients for the sauce and set aside.

Heat 1 tablespoon of oil in a large frying pan over a high heat. Add the green beans and stir-fry for around 3–5 minutes, until beginning to char.

Turn down the heat slightly and add the garlic. Stir-fry until golden. You may need to add a little more oil to stop the garlic burning.

Pour over the sauce, stir, and turn off the heat. Sprinkle with the toasted sesame seeds and serve immediately.

Stir-fried Cabbage with Chilli Butter

Serves: 4

Prep: 5 mins

Cook: 10 mins

- 1 tbsp neutral oil
- 1 medium hispi (also known as pointed) or sweetheart cabbage (approx. 500g), core removed, quartered lengthways and cut into 4–5cm pieces
- 30g/2 tbsp butter
- 1–2 tsp chilli bean paste (see tip and page 14)
- 2 tsp honey
- 3 tbsp water

Delicious with

Chinese 5-spice Prawns (page 104)

Sticky Chilli Salmon (page 102)

Next-level cabbage, here we come. First charred to add a smokiness, the cabbage is then finished with butter, chilli bean paste and honey, making it deliciously tender. The richness of the butter works beautifully with the chilli bean paste, resulting in this savoury, slightly spicy, and of course umami-packed dish. Perfect as a side or as part of a larger meal, but don't be surprised if you end up just eating it on its own – it really is that good!

Heat 1 tablespoon of oil in a large frying pan or wok over a high heat, and fry the cabbage for 3–4 minutes, stirring occasionally, until it starts to char.

Add the butter, chilli bean paste and honey, along with 3 tablespoons of water.

Combine well and stir-fry for a few more minutes, until the cabbage is cooked.

T I P

If you can't get hold of hispi or sweetheart cabbage, other cabbages such as Savoy, green or white can be used instead. You may have to adjust the cooking times accordingly.

T I P

The saltiness of chilli bean paste brands varies. I use Lee Kum Kee, which is less salty than some others. If using another brand, start off with 1 teaspoon – and add more if necessary.

Chilli & Garlic Charred Broccoli

Serves:	Prep:	Cook:
4	5 mins	7 mins

For the sauce
2–4 tsp chilli bean paste (see tip)
2 tbsp rice vinegar
2 tsp caster sugar
2–3 tbsp water

For the broccoli
1 tbsp neutral oil
300g tenderstem broccoli, cut into bite-size pieces

Delicious with
Sticky Chilli Salmon (page 102)
Soy & Star Anise Braised Chicken (page 182)

Broccoli is my go-to side vegetable. For simplicity and taste, I usually just char it on a high heat with a drizzle of oil and a pinch of salt. Even my kids love it. Here, I have elevated it with the addition of hot and garlicky chilli bean paste along with some vinegar for tang. Veggies never tasted so good!

Place the chilli bean paste, vinegar and sugar in a small bowl along with 2 tablespoons of the water, and combine. Set near the stove.

Heat 1 tablespoon of oil in a large frying pan or wok over a high heat, then add the broccoli. Stir-fry occasionally but don't move it too much – you want to develop a nice char.

Once the broccoli is just cooked (you want some bite), add the sauce. Reduce the heat slightly and bubble for a few moments. Taste the sauce, and if you need any more of the chilli bean paste, add it and combine. If on the other hand it is too thick or too salty, add the remaining tablespoon of water. Serve immediately.

 If you can't get hold of chilli bean paste, use 2 teaspoons each of sriracha and miso with ¼ teaspoon of chilli flakes.

 The saltiness of chilli bean paste brands varies. I use Lee Kum Kee, which is less salty than some others. If using another brand, start off with 2 teaspoons and add more if necessary (see page 14).

extras

Shanghai Spring Onion Flatbread

Serves:
3–4

Prep:
15 mins

Cook:
8–10 mins

250g self-raising flour
1½ tsp baking powder
½ tsp fine salt
¼ tsp Chinese 5-spice
2 tbsp neutral oil, plus more to fry and brush
150ml water
4 spring onions
2 tbsp raw sesame seeds

Delicious with
Malaysian Chicken, Spinach & Chickpea Curry (page 78)
Aromatic Coconut Salmon Curry (page 66)

Based on a popular Chinese street food – Shanghai scallion flatbread – this cheat's version eschews yeast in favour of self-raising flour and baking powder for a quicker, yet still entirely delicious bread. The method might sound complicated but once you do it, all will make sense. The end result is a crispy, golden brown, warm bread, layers of sweet spring onions and a hint of Chinese 5-spice. I can't tell you how moreish it is! I love it dipped into the sauce of one of my curries, but could equally demolish several wedges on their own!

Place the flour, baking powder, salt and Chinese 5-spice in a mixing bowl and combine. Pour over the oil and the water, using a wooden spoon to mix as you go. Use your hands once the dough starts to come together. You may need a little more water if it seems too dry.

Turn out the dough and knead for a minute or two, until it springs back when you touch it. Cover and leave to rest.

Thinly slice the spring onions. If you have time to leave the dough for 10 minutes, great – if not, proceed to the next step.

Roll out the dough on a floured surface into a roughly rectangular shape, approx. 3–4mm thick. Brush with 2 teaspoons of oil, then scatter over the spring onions. Roll up the dough lengthways to form a tight log, then roll it into a coil. Tuck the end underneath.

Roll the dough into a circle, approximately 20cm wide and 1½cm thick. Sprinkle over half the sesame seeds, patting them into the dough as you go. Turn over the dough and repeat on the other side.

Heat a drizzle of oil in a frying pan over a medium heat. Place the dough in the pan and cook for around 4–5 minutes, until crispy and golden. Be careful not to burn it – you may need to reduce the heat slightly. Turn over the flatbread, adding a drizzle more oil to the pan. Cook for a further 4–5 minutes, until the second side is also golden, crispy and cooked through. When tapped it should sound slightly hollow. Cut into wedges and serve immediately.

Tangy Pickled Cabbage

Serves: 4   Prep: 5 mins   Cook: 0 mins

300g Chinese or napa cabbage, thinly sliced
1 clove of garlic, crushed
½ tsp chilli flakes
1 tsp sugar
½ tsp fine salt
4 tbsp rice vinegar

Delicious with
curries, stir-fries, Thai soups, noodles
Chiang Mai Curried Noodles with Crispy Coconut Tofu (page 82)
Fiery Southern Thai Dry Pork Curry (page 76)
Korean Sweet Potato, Chickpea & Spring Green Stew (page 164)

My mum often buys me little tins of pickled mustard greens when she visits her local Asian supermarket. Known as pak dong, they are a traditional condiment in Thai cuisine. Their sour, salty and slightly sweet flavour works incredibly well with many Thai dishes, helping to balance out heat and richness. Mustard greens are not always easily available here in the UK, so I wanted to create a recipe with a similar flavour profile that you could make at home. This tangy pickled cabbage works brilliantly in its place.

See photo on page 193.

Place all the ingredients in a mixing bowl and combine well, taking a minute or two to work everything into the cabbage.

Place in the fridge and leave for at least 30 minutes before eating. Keeps in the fridge for approximately 1 week in a sealed, clean container.

TIP: If you can't get hold of Chinese or napa cabbage, white cabbage will also work.

TIP: Although best enjoyed after at least 30–60 minutes, so it has time for the flavours to meld and the cabbage to soften slightly, you can also eat it immediately for a fresher, crunchier experience.

Soy & Sesame Cucumber Pickle

Serves:	Prep:	Cook:
4	5 mins	0 mins

2 tbsp light soy sauce

2 tbsp rice vinegar

1 tsp toasted sesame oil

2 tsp sugar

2 cloves of garlic, crushed

½ tsp chilli flakes (add more if you like it hot)

1 cucumber, quartered lengthways and cut into bite-size pieces

Delicious with

Korean Chicken & Kimchi Rice Traybake (page 122)

Sticky Hoisin Beef (page 136)

Chilli Peanut Beef Rice Bowl (page 140)

A quick Korean-inspired pickle to serve on the side. Feel free to adjust the chilli flakes as needed.

See photo on page 193.

Place all the ingredients apart from the cucumber in a bowl and stir to dissolve the sugar. Add the cucumber and combine.

Store in the fridge until needed. Best eaten the day it's made.

Easy Homemade Hot Sauce

Makes:
1 small jar

Prep:
5 mins

Cook:
10–15 mins

- 150g mild red chillies, chopped
- 6 cloves of garlic, roughly chopped
- 1 tsp salt
- 200ml white wine or apple cider vinegar
- 100ml water
- 2 tbsp sugar

This is the first hot sauce I ever made and is actually the basis for The Woolf's Kitchen Hot + Sour sauce. It's a great multi-purpose condiment, as delicious on noodles, eggs and rice dishes as it is on wraps and tacos. You could also use it in place of sriracha in recipes – just be mindful that it is a little sweeter, so you'll want to taste and adjust the seasoning of the dish accordingly.

See photo on page 192.

Put all the ingredients into a small saucepan and bring to a simmer. Lower the heat and cook for 10–15 minutes, until the chillies and garlic are soft.

Leave to cool for a few minutes, then transfer to the jug of a stick blender or a small food processor and blend until smooth. Taste and add any extra sugar or salt if needed, while still warm.

Pour into a sterilized container and store in the fridge for up to 3 months.

T I P Mild chillies can vary in heat – sometimes they have none whatsoever, and other times they blow your head off. I like to keep the seeds in, but if you like it milder, please deseed. If you want to further temper the heat, you can add a chopped red pepper to the mix.

T I P You might want to use gloves to chop the chillies – otherwise, be careful where you put your fingers in the hours after!

Quick Radish Pickle
with Garlic, Ginger & Chilli

| Serves:
4–6 | Prep:
10 mins | Cook:
0 mins |

A quick peppery pickle to liven up your mains.

See photo on page 192.

200g pink radishes, thinly
 sliced

¼ tsp fine salt

1 tsp sugar

1 small clove of garlic,
 crushed

1 tsp grated fresh ginger
 (approx. 2cm)

¼ tsp chilli flakes

1 tbsp rice vinegar

Delicious with

Chilli Sesame Chicken Stir-fry
 (page 128)

Stir-fried Curry Noodles
 (page 92)

Combine the ingredients well in a bowl. The pickle can be served immediately, but keeps for a few days in the fridge in an airtight container.

T
I
P

The radishes do lose their crunch over time, so if you prefer a crunchier texture, they are best eaten the same day.

Easy Chilli Oil with Bits

Makes:
1 small jar

Prep:
5 mins

Cook:
3 mins

- 2 tbsp chilli flakes
- 4 fat cloves of garlic, finely chopped
- 1 tsp caster sugar
- ¼ tsp fine salt
- 150ml neutral oil
- 25g shop-bought crispy onions

For those of you who don't know, crispy chilli oil is my obsession! I started making it a few years ago and thought it was so good, I had to share it with the world – and so The Woolf's Kitchen Chilli Crunch was born.

Not only do I dollop it on anything and everything from eggs to noodles and even toasties, but it's also one of my favourite ingredients for stir-fries, sauces, and more. I wanted to give you a cheat's recipe so you always have some to hand.

Making crispy chilli oil (also known as chilli crisp) usually involves frying copious amounts of sliced garlic and onion until crispy – which, let's face it, can be pretty time-consuming. This version uses shop-bought crispy onions instead, for a much quicker, easier fix. They will soften over time but will still be delicious!

See photo on page 193.

Put the chilli flakes, garlic, sugar and salt into a large heatproof bowl or jug.

Heat the oil in a pan on medium-high until hot (a wooden chopstick or a piece of garlic will fizz if you put it in). Carefully pour the oil on to the chilli mix and stir. Leave to cool.

Place the crispy onions in a pestle and mortar and gently crush to make the pieces a little smaller. Once the oil is cool, add the onions to the mixture and combine. Taste and add any extra salt or sugar as needed. Store in a sterilized jar. Will keep for up to 4 weeks in the fridge.

Sriracha Sesame Coconut Sprinkle

Makes: approx. 10 servings

Prep: 5 mins

Cook: 10 mins

40g desiccated coconut
20g raw sesame seeds
10g shop-bought crispy onions
¼ –½ tsp caster sugar
¼ tsp chilli flakes (optional)
sea salt flakes
1 tsp neutral oil
2 tbsp sriracha

A little magic dust to add some extra excitement to your dishes. Similar to my Peanut Serundeng in Dominique's Kitchen, *this instead uses sesame seeds and crispy onions for crunch, and sriracha for heat and flavour. Delicious sprinkled over stir-fries, noodles, salads, eggs and more.*

Don't forget to read the cooking tip below!

See photo on page 192.

Mix together the coconut, sesame seeds, crispy onions, ¼ teaspoon of sugar, chilli flakes and a pinch of salt in a small bowl.

Heat the oil in a frying pan over a medium heat, and when hot, tip in the coconut mixture. Add the sriracha, and stir to coat.

Reduce the heat to medium-low and fry for around 5 minutes, stirring constantly. You want to toast the coconut and dry out the sriracha, but be careful not to overcook – when you press the mixture with the back of the spoon it should feel less soft and slightly drier than it did when you first started cooking.

Remove from the pan immediately (otherwise it will carry on cooking).

Place on a plate to cool down and crisp up. Taste and add a pinch of sea salt and the remaining ¼ teaspoon of sugar if necessary. Once cold, place in an airtight container. Keeps for up to a month.

TIP It's vital not to overcook the coconut or it will taste burnt. It is better to underdo it than overdo it, as you can always fry it for another minute if you need to. The sriracha does make it hard to see when the coconut changes colour, but don't let it go fully brown. Be aware that the coconut won't fully crisp up until it cools down out of the pan.

sweets

Soy Sauce Chocolate Pots

Serves: 4–6

Prep: 5 mins

Cook: 5 mins

Chilling: + 2 hours

3 digestive biscuits
200g milk chocolate, chopped
150ml double cream
50ml milk
1 tsp light soy sauce

The idea of mixing soy sauce with chocolate might sound a little out there, but believe me when I say it works! The combination has been around for a while and is akin to using miso – in fact, my recipe for Miso Chocolate Fridge Cake in Dominique's Kitchen *is one of my most popular. You don't taste the soy itself, but it lends a slightly salty umami flavour that balances out the sweetness of the chocolate, creating an almost caramel effect. Rich and luxurious, yet incredibly easy and bound to impress your guests!*

Place the digestives in a bowl and crush with a rolling pin. Set aside.

Place the chocolate in a heatproof bowl. Heat together the cream and milk in a small pan over a medium-low heat. Bring to a simmer, turning off the heat just before it boils. Pour the milk over the chocolate and leave for a minute, then stir to combine. Add the soy sauce. The mixture should be silky smooth.

Divide the crushed digestives between 4–6 ramekins or espresso cups. Pour in the melted chocolate and leave to cool, then place in the fridge for around 2 hours to set.

Sesame & Stem Ginger Ice-Cream Sandwich

Serves:
4

Prep:
5 mins

Chilling:
6 hours or
overnight

300ml double cream
200g condensed milk
60g tahini
60g stem ginger, finely
chopped

To serve (optional)
brioche rolls, toasted
salted caramel sauce
2 gingernut biscuits and/or
1 packet of sesame snaps,
crushed
a handful of salted peanuts,
chopped

I love the playfulness of an ice-cream sandwich. Popular across the world, including much of Asia, there are as many variations as there are flavours. Inspired by a memorable treat I enjoyed at Chatuchak Weekend Market in Bangkok many years ago, this cheat's no-churn ice-cream combines nutty tahini with chewy bits of stem ginger for an indulgent dessert. It takes just a few minutes to make and requires minimal effort, with the ginger added after a couple of hours to prevent it from sinking to the bottom.

Of course, serving it as a sandwich is entirely optional – the ice-cream is just as delicious scooped into a bowl and eaten with a spoon!

Place the cream, condensed milk and tahini in a bowl. Using an electric whisk, beat the mixture for 2–3 minutes on high, until thickened and lines hold their shape.

Pour into a freezable container and freeze for 2 hours, until slightly set. Remove and stir in the stem ginger.

Put back into the freezer for 4 more hours or overnight, until set.

To serve, remove from the freezer a few minutes before using, then scoop into warm brioche rolls, drizzled with the salted caramel sauce and sprinkled with the topping of your choice.

Creamy Coconut
& Vermicelli Pudding

Serves:	Prep:	Cook:
4	5 mins	10 mins

1 x 400ml tin of coconut milk
200–300ml water
4 tbsp soft brown sugar
sea salt flakes
100g vermicelli rice noodles
splash of milk (optional)

For the brown sugar syrup
3 tbsp brown sugar
1½ tbsp water

To serve
1 mango, cut into small
  cubes

My mum occasionally used to make sticky rice for us as kids, but it was quite an involved process which included soaking the rice for hours. I wanted to create a dessert that had those flavours, but one that I could whip up at a moment's notice. Using vermicelli rice noodles, this dish cooks in super-quick time and has all the rich coconut deliciousness of the original, transporting me to a Thai island whenever the urge takes me!

Put the coconut milk and 200ml of water in a large saucepan over a medium heat. Stir in the sugar and a couple of pinches of salt and bring to a simmer.

Roughly break up the rice noodles as you add them to the pan. Simmer on a medium-low heat for about 4–5 minutes, until cooked, stirring occasionally. Use a pair of scissors to cut the noodles into small pieces. If you prefer the texture to be slightly looser, add a little more water. You could also add a splash of milk for extra creaminess, if desired.

Meanwhile, place the brown sugar and water in a small pan and stir to dissolve the sugar. Bubble for 2 minutes or so, until it becomes syrupy.

To serve, divide the noodles between four bowls, spoon over the brown sugar syrup and top with the mango.

TIP The noodles will absorb the liquid even after cooking, so add a little extra water to loosen if necessary. You could also add a splash of milk for extra creaminess but taste first!

Tamarind Toffee Apple Pudding

Serves: 6–8

Prep: 15 mins

Cook: 35–40 mins

140g butter, softened
100g caster sugar
2 eggs
100ml milk
140g self-raising flour
5 dessert apples, (approx. 600g), peeled and thinly sliced

For the sauce
120g soft brown sugar
4 tbsp tamarind paste (see pages 20–21)
250ml boiling water
4 tbsp coconut flakes/chips

To serve
ice cream

How I love an apple pudding! Here I've given the classic British dessert, apple sponge, a saucy tamarind twist. The tamarind itself is subtle but lends a fruitiness and tang to the sweet toffee apples.

This self-saucing pudding involves pouring a mixture of boiling water, sugar and tamarind over the batter and apples. Don't be alarmed by the way it looks (and don't be tempted to touch or mix it either). The liquid will miraculously make its way to the bottom, creating a sticky sauce, while the coconut chips and top will become golden.

Preheat the oven to 180°C/160°C fan/gas mark 4.

Beat the butter and sugar together using an electric beater until they become creamy. Beat in the eggs, followed by the milk. Mix in the flour and combine.

Arrange the apples over the base of a large oven dish (approx. 20cm x 27cm). Spoon over the mixture and level the top.

Mix the soft brown sugar, tamarind and water together in a jug. Once the sugar has dissolved, pour evenly over the batter. Scatter the top with the coconut and place in the oven for 35–40 minutes, until the top is golden and the batter is cooked through (a skewer inserted should come out clean).

Delicious served with ice cream.

White Chocolate, Miso & Coconut Pots

Serves: 4–6

Prep: 5 mins

Cook: 3 mins

Chilling: approx. 2 hours

200ml coconut cream

2 tsp white miso paste

200g white chocolate, chopped

To serve

fresh raspberries

These indulgent little pots are a crowd-pleaser, perfect for easy entertaining. The salty miso balances out the sweetness of the white chocolate, which in turn works beautifully with the velvety coconut cream. Raspberries add freshness and tartness to cut through, but mango or pineapple would be just as delicious.

Place the coconut cream and miso in a saucepan over a medium to medium-low heat. Stir to dissolve the miso (I find a small whisk helps). Add the white chocolate and stir.

Once melted, pour into four ramekins. Allow to cool slightly, then place in the fridge for around 2 hours or until set.

Delicious served with fresh raspberries.

T
I
P

Any leftover coconut cream can be frozen, or added to curries or smoothies for extra creaminess.

Sticky 5-Spice Cherry Bruschetta

Serves: 4

Prep: 10 mins

Cook: 10–15 mins

For the cherries
300g frozen cherries
4 tbsp soft brown sugar
½ tsp Chinese 5-spice
(see tip)
1 tbsp water

For the bruschetta
150g cream cheese
1 tbsp icing sugar
8 slices of ciabatta

A fun twist on a cheesecake, this cheat's dessert is ready in a fraction of the time. The frozen cherries, infused with a subtle hint of Chinese 5-spice, develop a gorgeously jammy texture that pairs beautifully with the rich cream cheese and crunchy toasted ciabatta. Delicious!

Place the ingredients for the cherries in a pan and heat on medium-high. Stir to dissolve the sugar, then bring to the boil. Reduce the heat slightly and bubble for around 5–10 minutes, until it becomes syrupy – the sauce should be able to coat the back of a metal spoon without running off easily. Set aside to cool. The cherries can be served either warm or cold.

In a bowl, mix together the cream cheese and icing sugar. Toast the ciabatta either in a toaster or under the grill, until nice and crunchy.

To serve, spread the cream cheese over the ciabatta and top with the cherries. Best eaten immediately.

TIP
If you don't have ciabatta, use baguette (you may need more than 8 slices, depending on the thickness) or sourdough (cut larger slices in half).

TIP
Please make sure you use Chinese 5-spice that does not have added garlic or onion powder (the ones labelled 'seasoning' tend to). Alternatively, you can use 2–3 whole star anise in its place.

Korean-style Chocolate & Coconut Stuffed Pancakes

Makes:
4

Prep:
15 mins

Cook:
10 mins

For the dough
200g self-raising flour
½ tsp fine salt
125ml water

For the filling
150g chocolate spread
35g desiccated coconut

To fry
1 tbsp neutral oil

Inspired by the Korean street food snack hotteok – a pancake typically filled with brown sugar, cinnamon and chopped nuts – this recipe combines chocolate spread with coconut for the most heavenly mouthful.

Completely different to your usual fluffy American variety of pancake, these are more like a stuffed flatbread if anything. Sealing the pancakes can seem fiddly at first, but you will speed up once you get the hang of it.

Combine the flour and salt in a mixing bowl. Add the water and mix. Once the dough starts to come together, tip it out on to a floured surface and knead for 2 minutes. Cover and set aside.

Spoon the chocolate spread into a small bowl. Place the coconut in a small frying pan over a medium heat and cook for a couple of minutes, until lightly golden, stirring frequently. Add the coconut to the bowl of chocolate spread and combine.

Divide the dough into 4 pieces. Take a ball of dough and flatten it into a circle approx. 13cm in diameter. Place 2 level tablespoons of the chocolate mixture in the centre, then lift up the dough and put it in the centre of your palm. Cup your hand around the dough and use your thumb and fingers to press the edges together, to enclose the centre. Make sure to pinch the edges tightly, to ensure it is completely sealed. Place seam side down and gently flatten with your fingers. Round the edges with your palms. Repeat with the remaining dough.

Heat 1 tablespoon of oil in a large non-stick frying pan over a medium heat. Place the pancakes in the pan, seam side down, and cook for 3–4 minutes on each side, until golden and the sides of the pancakes are cooked. If the pan gets too hot, reduce the heat slightly.

Wait for a minute for them to cool down, then devour!

TIP

Use level tablespoons of chocolate spread in your pancakes (rather than heaped), to avoid them bursting.

Index

Acknowledgements

I'm still pinching myself over the fact that I've had the opportunity to write not just one but two cookbooks. There are so many people involved in the whole process from start to finish who have made this all possible.

First and foremost, this book wouldn't have happened without Louise Moore at Penguin Michael Joseph – I can't thank you enough for your warmth and wise words, for supporting me from the beginning and for having such confidence in me. I hope I've done you proud.

The whole team at Penguin have been incredible – they not only helped make *Dominique's Kitchen* a success but have expertly guided me through the creation of book two. Huge thanks to my publisher Dan Hurst for your brilliant and creative ideas, for all your input and advice and for being a valued recipe tester! And to the rest of the team for your hard work, Aggie Russell, Sarah Fraser, Kallie Townsend and Hattie Evans. A big thank you also to Annie Lee for your editing prowess!

To my wonderful photographer Uyen Luu for nailing my vision, and her assistants Laurie Noble and Martyna Wlodarska; to the food team, Lucy Turnbull and her assistants Immy Mucklow, Freya Matchett and Kristine Jakobsson for making the food look even better than I could have hoped. Thanks to Heather Marnie for your top make-up skills. A big thank you to my agent Martine Carter for your all your hard work, wisdom and support.

To all my recipe testers – you've been amazing and I couldn't have done this without you! Sheila Lewis (special thanks to Sheila for being a superstar and also manning my *Dominique's Kitchen* Cookbook Club Facebook group as well!), Lotte Debell, Jess Strong, Lisa Wilson Hardy, Ali & Joe Malone, Marianne & Ian Mitchell, Marcelo Prado, Christian Spry, Melissa Ng, Robert Ng, Katy Fattuhi, Hilary & Doug Grierson, Caroline & Rob Bleaney, Jess Feller,

Torie True, Valeria & Robert Hart, Marni Xuto, Cherie Jones, Rachel Redlaw, Lyndsay Holden, Connie Cullum, Ione Walder, Dan Hurst and Aggie Russell.

Thank you to Misako Nishimura and Vy Cutting for sharing your recipes and helping me with my research, and Melissa Ng, Robert Ng, Marni Xuto, Cherie Jones and Fernando Granzotto for all your food advice. To Toni Koppel, thank you so much for always championing me!

As always, it takes a village to raise a family, and I couldn't have written a book whilst juggling three kids and a small business without my own family to support me. Mum and Michael, I thank you from the bottom of my heart for being there pretty much 24/7 to help with the kids and house (I can't imagine how chaotic things would be without you!). Mum, you also excelled as chief recipe taster – someone whose palate I trust and who I could rely on to be as blunt as needed! Heartfelt thanks to my dad for regularly making a one-hour-plus journey here to take the kids out – it means so much. And to Bridget for looking after him! Big thanks to my brother Sean for your unconditional support and to my Auntie Dang for continuing to inspire my cooking.

I owe a debt of gratitude to my in-laws Joyce and Lawrence Mitchell for being the biggest cheerleaders I could have hoped for. Thank you for spreading the word – I owe my Scottish success all to you!

Finally, big love goes to my husband Gordon and three little monkeys Logan, Florence and Grace. Gordon – the rock behind our family, always supporting me in following my dreams. And kids – thank you for always keeping me on my toes and being willing to try my creations – it's such a delight to feed you!

Dominique

PENGUIN MICHAEL JOSEPH

UK | USA | Canada | Ireland | Australia
India | New Zealand | South Africa

Penguin Michael Joseph is part of the Penguin Random House group
of companies whose addresses can be found at
global.penguinrandomhouse.com

Penguin
Random House
UK

First published 2024
001

Set in Kobe, ITC Avant Garde Gothic Pro and Memphis
Colour reproduction by AltaImage Ltd
Printed and bound in China by Toppan Leefung

The authorized representative in the EEA is Penguin Random House
Ireland, Morrison Chambers, 32 Nassau Street, Dublin D02 YH68

A CIP catalogue record for this book is available
from the British Library

ISBN: 978-1-405-95792-2

www.greenpenguin.co.uk

MIX
Paper | Supporting
responsible forestry
FSC® C018179

Penguin Random House is committed to a
sustainable future for our business, our readers
and our planet. This book is made from Forest
Stewardship Council® certified paper.